The Highest Life

BOOKS BY GENE EDWARDS

A Tale of Three Kings
The Divine Romance
The Prisoner in the Third Cell
Revolution: The Story of the Early Church
The Inward Journey
The Highest Life
The Secret to the Christian Life
Letters to a Devastated Christian
Dear Lillian
Climb the Highest Mountain
Preventing a Church Split

The Chronicles of the Door
The Beginning
The Birth

THE HIGHEST LIFE

GENE EDWARDS

Tyndale House Publishers, Inc.
Wheaton, Illinois

Library of Congress Cataloging-in-Publication Data

Edwards, Gene, 1932-
    The highest life / Gene Edwards.
        p.   cm.
      ISBN 0-8423-1351-6
      1. Spiritual life. I. Title.
      BV4501.2.E3115   1993
      248.4—dc20   92-42636

Printed in the United States of America

99   98   97   96   95   94   93
9   8   7   6   5   4   3   2   1

In Memoriam

This book is dedicated to an illiterate Louisiana French Cajun—a tough, rough-and-tumble oil field roughneck known to everyone only by the name Blackie. Though wholly without any formal schooling, he was an organic genius and the most brilliant leader of men I have ever known, as well as the most awesome man it has ever been my experience to encounter. He was also someone I loved very deeply and who, in his own inimitable style, loved me. And though, from my earliest recollection, I have always known him as Blackie, it was ordained by a sovereign and gracious God that I also have the singular privilege to know this man as *Dad*.

To my father,
J. C. EDWARDS

Papa, I will hold the memory of you in my heart and in my tears—until that day when we shall see him face to face whom we shall both call **our Father.**

Contents

Introduction

This is the first of two books on the deeper Christian life.

Where shall we begin such a sojourn? I would like to invite you to return with me to eternity past! That should be far enough back to make this book an introduction!

Return with me to the age before creation! Before the creation of things seen. Even before things unseen.

What do we find in this most primordial of all ages? We find God. Nothing else. Just God.

I pose a question here that goes to the very heart of having a deeper walk with the Lord. The question is unusual and may catch you by surprise: *"What* is God?"

An odd question, is it not? And note that the question is, *"What* is God?" not *"Who* is God?"

What is rain? Water. What is a statue? Stone. What is a table? Wood. And *what* is God? He is *spirit.* You might say, from the viewpoint of physics, His molecular structure is *spirit.* (Or He has *no* molecular structure because He is spirit.)

Now, dear reader, a very simple conclusion: If God is spirit, then it follows that the highest of all states is spirit. The first state and the highest is spirit—certainly higher than anything that is *not* spirit.

Next, please observe that "spirit" is *invisible*. Now we must conclude invisible is higher than visible. The spiritual and the invisible are *before* (and higher than) the physical and the material.

In His first and highest state, your Lord is spirit and invisible. Therefore He is nonmaterial, nonvisible, nonphysical. What else is He?

The key to understanding so much of what is important to a deeper walk with Christ is to return to that *primordial* age and learn that He is also *life*.

Which life? Well, in that primordial era He was the *only* life. So we may say *at that time* He was the *only* life. Later, when He creates, there *will be* other forms of life. But when that moment comes, which will be the *highest* form of life?

The answer is clear and simple. The eternal God is, was, and ever shall be the highest form of life.

So, if you ever hear *God* talking about *life,* He can only be referring to one particular life form. The highest life form. *His* life form. Keep that in mind. (Especially when reading a book written by a man named John.)

Now to our last question. And if this question strikes you as a bit strange, be patient; for it could eventually be one of the most important questions ever asked of a believer seeking to know Christ better.

> When God gets up in the morning, by what life does He live?

When God gets up in the morning and begins doing whatever it is that God does, is it conceivable that He lives by mineral life, vegetable life, or *human* life? Not likely.

When God gets up in the morning, He lives by means of His own life. He lives by *divine life!* The engine of God's daily living is His own divine life. When He speaks of this fact, He refers to *Life,* rather than calling it the highest life, simply because it is the only life that has been around forever. He is referring to *His* life whenever He says *Life.*

God, who is spirit and is invisible, is also Life. He is the highest life. And when He gets up in the morning, He lives by *that* life, the highest life, *His* life. Whatever God does, He does by the dynamics of divine life.

Can anyone else, *has* anyone else, ever gotten up in the morning and lived by divine life? Has a tree ever done that, or a bird, or an angel? Or a human? Can anyone, except God, get up in the morning and live by means of the highest form of life? Or is this means of living reserved exclusively, totally, utterly for God alone?

As we close this simple introduction, let it be pointed out that God's life has another name. There is a word given to God's life that describes this fact: God has eternal life. (No, that is not totally accurate. God *is* Eternal Life.)

Go back as far as you like, and God will be there. Go forward as far as you can, and God will be there.

In the New Testament you will find just about all of the people who played on center stage using the words (1) *Life,* (2) *Eternal Life,* and (3) *Spirit.* They are speaking of *Him* . . . and of *His* life. Eternal Life is the exclusive franchise of God alone, and it is what He lives by!

> There never was
> when God was not;
> There never will be
> when God will not be.
> And in His daily living,
> He lives the *"victorious life"*
> by means of His own life.

Now, summing up. *Spirit* and *spiritual* came first. Spirit and spiritual are higher and of greater importance. Material, physical, and visible (which came much later) are second-rate in comparison to spirit, spiritual, and the invisibles. Remember: God, by nature, *is* spirit. And He (and He alone) is the highest of all life forms.

In all spiritual realms in all ages of the eternals, in every space-time continuum, on any and every level of any continuum that exists, your Lord is the highest life form, and He lives by means of this highest life.

It will not surprise you, then, that He tends to favor words describing Himself, His conduct and His habitat—words that communicate to you things about Himself and His nature. He is telling you about His experience. No philosophy or theology here. Just God's own habitat, life form, His molecular structure, *His* experience. In order to convey things about Himself, He seems to be partial to words such as:

> Spirit
> The Unseen
> The Invisible

Divine Life
The Spirituals
The Eternals
Life
Eternal Life

The last two words appear to be His all-time favorites. But these words do not tell us about our Lord only. These words came into our vocabulary because they have a great deal to do with *our* walk with Christ.

When we began this book, there was God and nothing else. Remember? This, too, will aid us in understanding the deep things of God. On our way to understanding the deeper Christian life, we began in eternity past *before* anything was created. Let's move forward now and see just what it was He *first* created.

PART 1

ONE

Where the Deeper Christian Life Has Its Roots

The first creating act of the eternal God should come as no surprise. He created a spiritual realm. This realm matched the nature and substance of God. It was an invisible, spiritual, nonmaterial, nonphysical realm that He created. This realm matched Him. As water matched fish and air matched birds . . . the natural, organic habitat of God reflected His organic nature—spiritual and invisible.

It will not surprise you that this realm is also nondimensional, for God is nondimensional. But what does that mean? It means you would have a very difficult time trying to measure Him or the place He lives. This realm has no "up" or "down," no height-length-depth. Or weight. Or size. Not that it is large. Or small. That *first* realm, the spirituals, is none of these. It is, well, nondimensional.

This invisible realm where God lives also has no time in it. This realm came into existence before space-time and is outside the measurements and concepts of time.

If that is not enough to give us a hefty headache, consider the fact that there is no *space* in this realm. Ingredients called *time and space* had not yet been "invented."

Space and time have to do with mass. (We are assured of this fact by no less a personage than Einstein.) *Mass* has to do with the material. The first (and quite invisible) realm has no material, no mass in it. *Physics* doesn't operate here.

The *other* realm:

> Invisible
> Free of time
> Nonmaterial
> Nondimensional
> Spiritual

Obviously, we have a struggle grasping all of those things because we never lived in a habitat with such odd features. You are a creature of space-time, of the dimensional and the physical. The other realm could swallow up every bit of the visible, physical realm, or it could fit comfortably inside your rib cage and you would suffer no ill effects. As I said, you and I simply cannot fully grasp such things.

One other odd feature of the first realm He created: You cannot get there from here. Travel in the fastest spaceship imaginable and travel in it *forever,* and still you will never get there. You can't travel to that realm from this realm. It's not "out there." The spiritual realm can only be reached by a *Door.* Yes, a Door. There is a Door between that realm and our realm. That Door is our only access to the *other* realm!

By the way, this fascinating place called the spirituals has another name. It is called "the heavenlies" or "heavenly places." That place is where God dwells.

Now that we know a little (very little!) about the spiritual realm, perhaps we can better understand the first life form that God ever *created.* Let's say that again. We are about to see the first *created* form of life. God's first creation of a life form took place in that other realm. And that particular form of life He created just happened to "fit" the spiritual realm. What, or *whom,* did He first create?

Angels!

Angels match their habitat. To some degree at least, they match their Creator, who also lives there. The realm where angels live is spiritual. And angels are *spirits.* Their realm is *invisible,* and angels are also, most decidedly, *invisible.* This realm is light, *and* angels also are robed in light. (Dear fellow earth mortal, do not ask me how one can be both clothed in light and invisible, for I have no idea.)

Angels *match* their environment: spiritual beings in a spiritual realm.

Angels also have something in common with their Creator. They are spirits. Their Creator is spirit, and they are spirit. (Except He is *the* Spirit.) Both life forms are spirit.

But one thing the angels do not have in common with their Lord: Angels are created. God is, well, *uncreated.* He has *eternal* life. No beginning, no end.

(When it comes to *His* life, the arrow of infinity points in *both* directions.) Angels only have *everlasting* life. They have a life form that does begin but never ends. (The arrow of infinity points in only one direction.) It is true that when God created angels, He started something that would not end, but they did *start!* They are *created* and have a definite point of beginning. *He,* on the other hand, never had a beginning. That is why we refer to *Him* as *Eternal Life.*

Now to the central question.

When angels get out of bed in the morning, or whatever it is that angels do, by what life do they live? The answer is obvious. Angels get up in the morning and live by angel life. The dynamics, the source, the engine of an angel's living is angelic life . . . *the angelic life form!* Angels live by the highest *created* life form.

Please note: Angels live by means of angel life. God lives by means of God's life. Angels do *not* live by God's life. Only God lives by means of the highest life. God *is* Eternal Life. Angels live by angelic life.

It is time for us now to introduce something very scientific: the biological chart. Do you remember your biology class in high school? There was a chart on the wall. At the bottom of the chart was a picture of grass, herbs, trees; then came fish and reptiles. On up the chart were pictures, each life form pictured being higher than the last. At the top of the chart was man. This was your introduction to biology. *Biology* defined is "the science and study of life."

Have you ever heard of *zoe*-ology? Well, neither have I, but *zoe* is a Greek word meaning "life," so we will use it to refer to heavenly life forms. If we combine biology and *zoe*-ology on the same life chart, then we can add two more forms of life to the chart. The *top* two! And the life form at the very top of this bio-*zoe* chart is God. He is the highest life! The highest form of life is God. Second-highest: angels. Third-highest: people.

From now on, I will use the term *biology*—the science of life—to include both bio-ology and *zoe*-ology. Keep that in mind wherever you see the word *biology*.

By the way, one of the main points of this book can be seen in a term often used by the judicial system and the medical world. Have you ever heard this question: "Who is the biological father?" Or, "The DNA test shows John Smith to be the biological father."

Keeping in mind both *bio*- and *zoe*-ology, we can ask, "Do you know your biological father?" When we include *zoe* in our "biology," then those of us who are believers have the right to say, "God is my 'biological' father." How dare we say this? Because we have His life in us. And that life is one with us.

Let us return, now, to our chart. Up until now, starting at the top of the chart, we have only two life forms on the chart. God's life and angel's life. (More life forms will be added to this "life chart.")

A pattern is developing here, is it not? Each life form that God creates lives by the engine of its particular form of life. Right?

Don't bet on it!

One last look at the angels. Not only are they spirits and invisible, but they travel *very* fast. They are also *neuter* (neither male nor female). They have everlasting life. There are about 100 million of them, and they share a common *created* life form.

Finally, and most important, angels are the highest created life form on our bio-*zoe* life chart. Higher than any other form of life *ever created*. They are the second-highest life form in the universe and the highest *created* form of life. They come in second only to the highest life, God Himself. Angels are a higher life form than man, so don't ever wrestle with one or you will surely lose. And let us hope none of them ever invade earth, for if they do, they will conquer us.

Now let us move to God's next act of creation, the creation of the *visible* realm. *Our* realm. In this realm, you will encounter a life form that breaks all

THE BIO-ZOE-OLOGICAL CHART

The Highest Life   GOD—Spirit (uncreated, eternal)
Second-highest Life   ANGELS—spirit (created, everlasting)
Third-highest Life   PEOPLE—soul, body, and spirit   *Unfallen Adam life*—soul, spirit, body   *Fallen Adam life*—fallen body, fallen   soul, deadened spirit   *Believers*—soul cleansed, spirit made   alive, fallen body
Fourth-highest Life   ANIMALS—soul and body
Fifth-highest Life   VEGETATION—body (no consciousness)

the biological rules, and, in so doing, causes a great deal of consternation and even stirs up a great deal of *mystery*.

TWO

Life Forms, Visible and Invisible

You can learn a great deal about where your Lord's ultimate interest lay by noticing how much time He spent creating and *where* He spent that time. The spiritual realm He created in short order. The physical realm, except for one small ball, took little over one day. He spent almost five days working on that small ball, which happens to be the little planet we live on. (We conclude, then, that His greatest interest lies here, among us.) All the stars, comets, pulsars, novas, galaxies, and all the other "nonliving" things took only a moment for your Lord to create. When He got down to the business of creating *living* things and especially *visible* living things, His creation work slowed down considerably.

Before God made anything that was both physical *and* living, He first made a *habitat* for living things to live in! Having finished the habitat, He began creating *visible* forms of life. And all these living creatures made their habitat on *this* little ball made of dirt and water.

As God first began to create life forms here on Planet Earth, He reversed His order of creation. *Here* He began at the bottom of the biological chart and went up. The Lord began by creating the *lowest* form of life. He created a form of life so low it had *no* consciousness. It was green stuff. Vegetation. The very bottom of the biological chart. This living green stuff was physical, it had mass; it belonged to, and obeyed, the laws of space-time. Visible, physical, dimensional. But unlike stars and comets, this green stuff was alive. Until the vegetation came along, nothing visible had also been *alive.*

Then came life that *truly* matched its place of habitation. As angels are invisible to match the invisible realm and are spirits to match the spiritual realm, now come creatures matching *this* realm.

First came forms of life with a measure (albeit a small measure) of consciousness. Sea life, that is, *fish!*

Next came a more complex form, one a little more conscious of itself and its surroundings. Sky life! Life that could fly. Fowls of the air. *Birds!* Next came *mammals.*

Enter, the *animals.* Just as invisible angels had spirits, the visible animals had *souls.* To say that animals have souls is to say that they can *think,* they can *choose,* and they have *emotions. Souls* go with this realm as *spirits* go with the other realm. The animals were not the highest expression of soul life, of course, but they do give us insight into soul life. Another being would soon be coming, after the animals, whose *soul* was as wondrous in this realm as an angel's *spirit* was in the invisible realm.

Note that animals were made of material, just as the visible realm is made of material. Their biological structure belonged within the jurisdiction of physics.

See, then, one difference between soul and spirit. Invisible angels, made of spirit, in a nonmaterial realm, contacted God and one another by means of their *spirits*. The visible animals, made of material and mass in a visible realm, communicated with *one another* by means of their souls. The animals were conscious of themselves and others, by means of their soulical natures.

Spirit is the life form that belongs to the invisible realm; *soul* is the life form that belongs to the physical realm.

We return to our chart. At the bottom is vegetation, with no consciousness. Then a series of creatures—fish, birds, and mammals—conscious of self and others. Then man, conscious of self, others, and also *conscious* of *God!* Then going up the chart, we move to the other realm to find angels. At the top of the chart, God . . . the highest life!

Creatures tend to match what they are made out of. Right?

Please note the last life form that God ever created. Man. And what of man?

Man belongs to the physical realm, so you would expect him to match his habitat. He was made of red clay, and that is definitely *physical*. Man will, therefore, be a body and soul, will he not? Just as animals are body and soul? And he will be confined to space-time. Right? And live in the jurisdiction reserved for the laws of physics, and be held captive here in this continuum just like the animals are—dimensional, visible, physical—limited to the mass-material dimensions of height, depth, and breadth? And unlike angels, he will be barred from access to the other realm. Like a horse or cow, he will be a citizen of this realm and this realm alone. Right?

Don't bet the family farm on it!

Contrary to what Socrates, Plato, Aristotle, and all philosophers and almost all theologians have ever taught, expect a big surprise. A surprise so big, we would be wise to give it an entire chapter.

There is one form of life that breaks all the rules.

THREE

The Creature from Two Realms

Friday is about to come to a close. God has created an invisible realm crowned by an invisible form of life called angels. Down here our little planet teems with all sorts of *visible* forms of life. The crown jewel of this realm awaits creation. God has reserved the unprecedented for last. True, the Living God is about to create only the *third*-highest of all forms of life, but it will be the *highest* form of life belonging to the visible realm. And this life form will be *unique* beyond all understanding.

As evening approaches, the Lord reaches His hands into the red-tinted sod and begins to fashion a most unusual-looking creature. When He chooses *dirt* to be man's biological structure, He signals to all creation that *this* particular creature belongs to

Planet Earth. As earth-man, his destiny will be tied wholly to the material realm and to this dusty orb. Man will be, as the cattle were, a body and soul.

Or, so it appeared.

Then came the unexpected! Man would not be made of substances from only *this* realm. God bent down over man and blew *some of the element of the other realm* into this red clay.

Man would therefore be . . .

Body, soul, and what?!

His body was earthen. For sure, his soul, by its very nature, belonged to this realm. Man's life was *soul* life, that is, *human* life. With his soul man would live and would interact with his species. With his soul he would also interact with the other living creatures, and with the planet itself. By means of his soul, man would set up a relationship with all things in the visible realm with which he would come in contact.

But this other thing that God had just placed in man! This *element* that came from the other realm, this *wind,* this *air,* this *breath* from the *other* realm, what was it? And what was its meaning? How would it alter man? And even more specifically, what was it for? What would it do?

Step back and look at man. He is *no longer* just of this earth, just of this realm. But neither can you say man is just of the other realm. He doesn't belong to the realm of the cattle, bird, and fish; neither does he belong to the realm of the angels. What is this man? This man who is body, soul, *and* spirit? Where does he belong on the biological chart?

What is man?

Man is creation's *only* hybrid.

Man is the *only* creature (and this includes even God) whose natural habitat is *both* realms.

And that fact, dear reader, has a great deal to do with your Christian walk!

Man is spirit, so he *belongs* to the invisible realm; he is of the spirituals. But he is also body and soul, so he *belongs* to the physical realm.

His habitat? Shall it be here or there? Or neither? Or the unthinkable—*both!*

Surely not!

A creature who is a citizen of both realms? With a right to both realms?

Endowed with elements from each of the two realms, man could have a line of communication with the creatures of the visible realm and yet be able to *see* the *unseen.* He could communicate with both realms! And even *live* in both realms. And *walk* in both realms! A line of communication to both realms!

Soul *and* spirit really are a formidable combination!

If he is of *both* realms, then *where* is man's *organic* habitat? Does he have two, or none? His natural habitat was earth. His natural habitat was also the heavenlies. He stood as one native to both the physical and the spiritual realms. He alone, among God and all creation, naturally belonged to both creations.

What, then, is man?

First of all, he is soul. He is *human* life. He is the third-highest life form in existence. He is the highest *visible* life form. He is certainly the highest form of life native to this planet. He is also the *second*-highest *created* life form. On the biological chart, he is listed just below the angels.

What is man?

God's life form is spirit. Angels' life form is spirit. Man's life form is soul (human life). Note that man's *spirit* is *not* a natural part of his life form. Rather, a man's spirit is an element of the spiritual realm abiding *within* man.

So what is man's biological structure? He is two-thirds of *this* realm (his body and soul) and one-third of the spiritual realm (his spirit).

Oh yes, our question. When man got out of bed in the morning, by what life did he live?

Man got out of bed every morning and lived by *human* life, by *soul* life. But that was *not* God's intention for man.

God had something else, far higher, planned for man. What? That answer must wait! Why? Because in the next chapters we must look upon the greatest tragedy ever to occur in all universal history. Perhaps the greatest aspect of this monstrous tragedy is that it just missed being the most *wonderful* event ever to occur in all universal history. Anyway, the Lord's Purpose in creating a creature native to both realms was thwarted (at least temporarily), as we shall now see.

FOUR

The Greatest Event That Never Happened

God had great plans for Adam. Those plans never came to fruition, but that shouldn't keep us from looking at what His plans were.

God's goal was all intertwined with a very special tree. Not just *any* tree. *The* tree. Specifically, the Tree of Life. As the scene opens, we see man standing before the tree. If he will just eat of the fruit of that tree, he will fulfill God's very Purpose in creating man.

And just what is that Purpose?

Man came very close to eating the fruit of this very special tree. What might have happened had he eaten of the Tree of Life? Or better, just what is it that is *in* the fruit of that tree? And what would that fruit have done *inside* man?

Note the name of the tree: the Source of *Life*. Not the source of a life, of *some kind* of life, but *the* life.

Do you remember *the* life—God's life!

That *tree* was located in a garden that was right here on this planet, but the wondrous tree was *not* native to this planet. It was not even native to this realm. *That* tree was an alien life form. Alien, yet here . . . on *our* planet.

From whence came this tree?

This alien tree contained nothing less than the *highest* form of life. Not the highest *created* life, but the highest of all forms of life, the very life by which God lives. *His* life is what pulsated within the fruit of *that* tree. Divine, *eternal life* was in its fruit. *That* was what man was poised to eat.

Let's put it another way: The life by which God lives was in that tree. And *man,* the third-highest form of life, was about to take *that* life into himself.

The highest life, indwelling a mere human! Do you recognize the implications?

Angels have only one form of life indwelling them. Cattle have only *one* form of life indwelling them. So also birds and fish. Even God has but one form of life within His being. True, it is the highest of all life forms, but it is, nonetheless, *one* life form. But what of man if he eats of this incredible fruit of this incredible tree? Obviously, he will have *two* forms of life dwelling in him! Two!

It was the greatest event that never happened!

But look at *some* of the implications. Man would have been able to get out of bed in the morning and have two life forms to live by! That is not all. One of the forms of life dwelling in him would have been native to *this* realm, and the other form of life dwelling in him would have been native to the *other* realm.

Right then, as man stood before *the* tree, he had an element from the spiritual realm and a life form from this realm. Eat from *that* tree, and he would have *two* life forms.

This means man would not only be able to contact *two* realms, he would have a habitat in two realms and have two forms of life to live by!

No other species, *not even God,* could make that claim!

As he poised before that tree, fruit in hand, man was about to become a wholly unique creature. All he needed to do was to take within his being the fruit of the tree of that higher life.

That is exactly what God desired man to do. Man was created with the *potential* of being a child of two realms, with two life forms, with the possibility of life in both realms—a child of this planet *and* a child of the other realm. *And* . . . the implications are that he would be able to *walk* in the physical realm and *walk* in the spiritual realm; and *live* in the physical realm and *live* in the spiritual realm. Maybe even at the same time!

> Man
> Of earth and of the heavenlies,
> Of clay and soul *and* of the invisibles and
>   spirit.
> A body and soul from this planet,
> A spirit from the other realm.
> Man
> A life form belonging to the material realm,
>   the human soul;
> A life form belonging to the spiritual realm,

God's own life in Man.
Man
A child of the visible,
A child of the invisible.
One who is wholly human,
And yet
One who has God's life in him.

What a glorious possibility! A soul with human life in it and a spirit with *the* life and *the* Spirit in it.

It never happened!

Man wandered off and ended up eating fruit from yet another tree. The *forbidden* tree.

Sadly, we must now pause to look at this other tree. After all, it is one of the key ingredients making up the biggest single mess of all time.

This forbidden tree was also alien to our planet. Like the Tree of Life, this forbidden tree held a form of life in it, but that life form was not the life of God. And the fruit of this tree could also *change* man; in fact, it did change man, but not for the better.

What has all this to do with you and your walk with the Lord? Well, you and I are who we are because of our parents. If your parents are giraffes, you end up being a giraffe. If your parents are human, then they give you human life, and sure enough you end up being *Homo sapiens!* You are a son (or daughter) of a man and woman. Because of this, you ended up being something called a *humanoid* life form.

You are what you are because of genetics. You end up somewhere on the biological chart solely because of your parents' genes. Your parents' DNA was passed on to you.

Up to this point in man's history, man does not have any of the "DNA" or genetics of God.* Consider this. If God should give to you His life, His DNA, His genetics, He would be your parent. And you would end up being a child of God. You would belong to His species. But so far, no such thing has happened.

In fact, such a thing *never* happened to Adam. It *almost* happened. Had it come about that man had actually received the DNA of God, it would have been the greatest event ever to take place. Instead, what *did* happen turned out to be the greatest tragedy ever to befall man and this creation. And, because Adam did pass on his DNA, his genetics, to you and to me, that tragedy also befell us. That tragedy played havoc with Adam's spiritual life. And with yours.

As we shall now see.

---

* DNA is the genetic code of man. Though God is spirit and is of another realm, where such things as DNA do not exist, nonetheless there is a genetics of God in the sense that, when He places this life in us, we receive His nature and character. The idea of God's DNA is used here, then, as an image, an instrument of communication.

FIVE

Creation's Greatest Tragedy

It was that other tree that launched the tragedy.

Two trees have played a key role in man's life. Neither was native to our planet; both *originally* came from the other realm.

The forbidden tree had pulsating within it a life form biologically superior to human life. The fruit of this tree carried within it the *second-highest* form of life. (It had in its fruit the highest *created* life.) What Adam did not know was this particular version of angelic life was *fallen* angelic life.

Fallen?

Yes. Angelic life that had tasted *final* knowledge. Angelic life that had had the actual *experience* of evil and good.

When this life form had its experiential encounter of evil and good, it fell from its high and heavenly estate. That "fallen" element of this tree now coursed out and flowed into the inmost being of Adam. Exactly *where* did this strange element go when it came into man?

It made its home *in* man's body. That marvelous and incredible body of Adam's was now *indwelt* by some foreign, fallen element. That element was superior to man, for it came from angel life. Later this element, this fruit of the forbidden tree, would receive a name. That name? Sin. Man's body had now become a container. A container for sin. This was the exact opposite of what God had planned. Man was supposed to be a container, yes, but not of sin! Man was supposed to contain eternal life!

When God gave him a spirit, He did so in order that man's spirit might be a container for the Holy Spirit, for divine life, for eternal life, for God's life, for the *highest* life. But that life never came into man's spirit. Man ended up, instead, with a *body* containing sin.

Having eaten the forbidden fruit instead of the fruit of the Tree of Life, man's body became the recipient of the fallen nature of an archangel.

Such a horrible presence in man's *body* had a profound effect on man's *soul*. Further, this terrible invasion was too much for man's human spirit. Man's spirit simply died to the spiritual realm. The spirit of man died to the realm from which it had come. When the human spirit died, man was suddenly cut off from the spirituals. For all practical purposes, Adam was ceasing to be a spiritual being. Experientially, he no longer belonged to the other realm. He could no longer see the unseen!

Essentially, man was now a creature of the physical realm *only*. Biologically, he was now a soul and body that was dragging around a spirit dead to its native habitat. Man did not lose his place on the biological chart. But instead of being just a fraction lower than angels, he had moved closer to being a one-realm creature, like the animals.

Nor did the tragedy end there. The tragedy *began* there. Man soon noticed that this body was aging. Nor was the soul immune to this ghastly catastrophe. The worst possible thing happened to his soul. The soul began to reach out and compensate for a spirit that was nonfunctioning. The soul tried to do double duty, carrying on its own functions and guessing at what his spirit had once done, and then trying to function in the spirit's place. The soul does a terribly poor job of this! That is decidedly *not* good news. The soul enlarged disproportionately. You might say the soul mutated.

Perhaps it was man's newly acquired learning experience—*his experiential knowledge of evil*—that caused this mutation. He had never *experienced* evil before. It is conceivable he might have known *of* evil by simply acquiring information about it, but now man had learned of evil by having *experienced* evil. (Some knowledge!)

This was to make man, including *you*, ultimately a knowledge seeker! You might even say the number one trait of the "old" man is the seeking of knowledge. His other most outstanding characteristic is trying to do good but ending up doing evil.

You see, the learning of evil experientially is only half the story. The other half is just as important but is often overlooked. Until now, man had been no more a creature of "good" than he had been a creature of "evil." He had *experienced* neither. Fallen man now had an experiential encounter not only with evil but also with *good*. This *tragedy* will henceforth hound *fallen man* every day of his life, as long as human life shall last.

Man's reaction to the experience of evil and the experience of good was bizarre. (Dear reader, please remember he ate of a tree with the knowledge of good in it just as surely as he ate of a tree with the knowledge of evil in it.) The bizarre result: Man would henceforth and forever hate evil and love good. He would despise doing evil and literally be euphoric when he managed to do good. But . . . he rarely managed to conquer the first nor do the second.

Man would henceforth take great notice of evil because he was so desperately enamored with wanting to do *good*. He would quite literally crave doing good. But as often as not he ended up doing evil instead. This sent him into greater and greater fits and pits of despondency. What this poor, pitiful creature didn't realize was his inward drive to do good and his inward drive to do evil *both* came from the same tree!

Man thought "doing good" was what would please God. His value system was distorted. He was mistaking "good" for "life." That simple but massive error drives his species to near madness every day.

Let us pause and survey the damage that has now been done to God's most magnificent creation.

Man had been of this realm but had the necessary internal parts to contact *both* realms and to claim the right to be of both realms. No longer. He is now a castaway. He is alone on this greatly damaged space vehicle called *terra. Inside him,* man is torn, even ravaged, by a mad pursuit of good and his feverish desire to forever abandon evil.

Man has two life forces at work in him. But one, his human life, is ultimately the slave of the other. The element of a fallen, alien life that is in his body is greater than he is, *one* biological classification higher than his life, to be exact.

For this reason, man's spiritual state might be seen from that point on as almost schizophrenic!

The fallen element of *another* life, working in his body, will cause him to sin. Sinning will cause him to feel terrible. He will be ashamed and begin writhing and contorting at his miserable conduct and evil deeds. He will then fall into despair. But after a while he will stand up, straighten himself, and will vow to never again do so dastardly a thing as to sin. To pacify an accusing conscience, he will go out and do something *good.* In this act of good he will reinform his mind that he is, basically, a decent person. (For this reason you will often find his descendants giving money to charity, doing penance, beating their chests in remorse, building an altar, or donating a new wing to the Notre Dame Cathedral.)

A few days later, this poor victim of some higher, darker life will go out and sin again. This desperate cycle repeats itself for as long as fallen man lives. "Good" will hound this pathetic species down the corridors of time until, in mercy, God causes the extinction of this species. Until that day, fallen man will remain sealed inside his dual, schizophrenic matrix, swinging desperately from good to evil and from evil to good.

Both inclinations (to sin *and* to be obsessed with "being good") come from the same source. This is a point he is totally incapable of grasping. And why not? He has never tasted the antidote to either good or evil. That antidote? Life! He sees in "good" his only hope of freedom and peace. In evil he sees the torment of everlasting enslavement. But in truth, it is both evil and good driving him on which, together, build his cage and forge his chains.*

Pushed out of the garden, a fallen species now sought to learn how to live on a fallen planet. The planet itself became inhospitable, and man has never really succeeded in living here. To this day, man's life outside his natural habitat is still primitive and barbaric.

But it was not the outward ecology of the fallen planet that was man's most maddening problem; it was what was going on *inside* man that was the source of his most terrible nightmares. He could never be sure which was a proper function of his soul and which was his soul usurping and perverting a function of his deadened spirit.

Understanding his deepest motives was now lost to man. *Now only God knew the true motives of man's heart.* And so it would forever be, until this fallen species is extinct.

His body was showing signs of becoming totally insensible to all the spiritual things it had once so beautifully exhibited.

---

* Call this state by its proper name: religion. Understand that fallen man is religious, *not* spiritual. This duel of good and evil in man is the author of both religion and legalism. See Addendum V for more on the roots of legalism.

More tragic still, the body's subservience to the soul was ending. The body had declared all-out war on the soul. And it was winning. Further, the body was magnifying all its senses. "Sense" was becoming "craving." These sensations were gaining control over man's soul. In a battle that knows no respite, the final outcome was in serious doubt.

Finally, this mutating, sensuous, warring body reached a point where it was no longer worthy to carry the name "body," and came to be known as "flesh."

Nonetheless, from somewhere deep within this once-glorious body there seemed to be a remembrance of things past. From deep within this conquered slave there rose a prayer that cried out for some unimaginable redemption. Earth, sun, moon, and stars—witnessing the enormity of their own fall and that of creation's greatest masterpiece—heard this prayer for redemption and joined in the wail. Man's soul, man's body, and earth's own bowels joined together in one mighty cry for some kind of salvation.

In the midst of this scene, the Tree of Life departed our planet and returned to the spiritual realm. Naked man, dragging a mutilated body and a dead spirit, took shelter on a fallen, convulsing planet. A fallen angel had a new slave to taunt. For how long? Forever?

Is man doomed to this ghastly nightmare for all eternity? Is there any hope for this man? The answer will surprise you.

And what has all this to do with your spiritual walk as a believer? On the biological chart we see a once-glorious species who has fallen drastically. The name of that species is *Homo sapiens.* You are listed among those belonging to that species. Just how damaged is this creature, spiritually? Is there any hope that man can ever recover from such a low spiritual state? Can he once more be one who walks in intimate fellowship with God?

The answer is *no.*

God will not only give up on this species, He will end it. His cure for fallen man is for the total extinction of that species.

That would appear to mean total hopelessness. Not really, though! God had a grander design! He would end this species and introduce a new species.

Right here on our planet God would introduce a totally new, completely different biological life form. Granted, this new species would look like the old species, but right there is where the similarity ends. *Inside,* these two life forms are very different.

Dear reader, you are about to meet a new biological entity, and the first motion in a brand-new creation.

PART 2

SIX

The Second Creature from Two Realms

His Father was from the other realm. His mother was of our planet. The question: Biologically, what is He?

He received the DNA and genes of divinity from His Father.* He is, therefore, *the* Son of God. He has eternal life within His being. No, He *is* eternal life! He has (and is) the highest form of life on the biological chart. He *is* divine; He is from the spiritual realm. On the other hand, He also has the DNA and biological genes of His mother. He has human life in Him.

So He has the highest life in Him *and* He has the third-highest life *in* Him. Which is He? The highest life or the third-highest life?

---

* See the discussion of "God's DNA" in chapter 4, page 23.

He is both. In point of fact, He is the *only* living being ever to have both these two life forms pulsating within Him.

Does He then belong to *this* realm or to the *other* realm? The physical, material, visible, molecular, temporal, dimensional, measurable, space-time universe made up of atoms and matter—is this His *home?* Or the spiritual, nonmaterial, invisible, permanent realm, the universe without dimension and without measurement—is that His *home?* The answer: He is *native* to both realms, and *both* are His natural habitat. He is at home in the eternals, where time (or nontime) goes in both directions. He roams the corridors of all events, in all directions. Until His birth in Bethlehem, He lived *in* the spiritual realm throughout all eternity past. Then for thirty-three years He was native to (and at home in) a small, limited, temporary, and visible realm where all events moved in but one direction. For all eternity past He lived in that realm. For thirty-three years He lived in this realm.

But more.

It appears He had the unique ability to live in both realms at the same time. While He lived in this, the physical realm, He was also, at the same moment, living in the spiritual realm.

And yet more.

He was also of royal blood . . . in both realms. In one He was the Son of the Lord God, the Creator of all things; and in our realm He was in line for the throne of a nation made up of God's people. The implications are staggering. If He conquered this planet and if His Father succeeded rule to Him in the invisible realm, He just might end up Lord and King of both realms. King of all kings, Lord of all lords.

But now to our key question.

While He lived on earth, when He got out of bed in the morning, by which life did He live? After all, Jesus Christ was on the biological chart twice! He had two parents, but each came from a different realm. Endowed with two life forms, He was, in the words of the greatest of all paradoxical statements, totally God and totally man. He was 100 percent a human being, yet God was His life; therefore, He was utterly divine. So when He got up in the morning, by which of those two lives did He live?

He lived primarily by divine life. He lived by the highest life. He was the only creature on this earth ever to do so. His third-class life lived in subjection to His first-class life! (His human life lived in subjugation to His divine life.) Here He was, living on this planet, in the likeness of human flesh, yet He lived by means of a biologically higher life.

A *man* who got up in the morning and lived by divine life; a man who lived by exactly the same life *God* lived by when *He* got up in the morning. This had never happened before.

But alas, this incredible man was the *only one* of His species. He was the most endangered of all species for there was but *one* of Him. And when He was murdered on a tree, that ended His race forever. There would never be a race here on earth with human life and divine life in it. There was to be only one being *on this planet* who would live by means of a higher life. It had never happened before; it would never happen again.

That statement is true, but God had an alternative. The alternative was so radical no one had ever thought of it.

God could absolutely destroy this creation, put an end to the old *Homo sapiens,* and then launch a whole new creation! If He did all that and *then* brought into existence a new biological species, well, *if* He did that, anything might be possible. Think of it. A species that was human—yet not really of Adam's species because Adam's species had been done away with. Human, yes, but also with the highest life embedded deep within.

Destroy the old creation? Have a brand-new creation? With a *new* species? A new species that could lay hold of the highest life?

Preposterous!

Utterly impossible? Don't be too sure! After all, you are dealing with the One who is the Creator of this realm, and He has been known to use some pretty desperate tactics to accomplish His *eternal Purpose.*

If there is even the slightest chance of such a species coming into existence, then it might behoove you to learn all you can about the biology, the sociology, the culture, and the values of Jesus Christ. Perhaps the wisest question you can ever ask, as a believer wishing to know your Lord more intimately, is this: Just exactly *how* did my Lord live by another life?

The answer requires a chapter of its own.

SEVEN

A Biological Look at a Certain Carpenter

The carpenter who lived in Nazareth looked some-what like *unfallen* Adam. Adam had the edge in outward appearance, but not internally. The internal differences were staggering! Adam had been, first and foremost, a living soul, then spirit, and lastly, body.

But what of the carpenter? He was *not* first a soul. And His spirit was not second to anything!! At the very center of His inmost being you find His spirit—the human spirit—alive! Complete. Functioning. But did not unfallen Adam have a spirit? Yes, and, like Adam, this carpenter's spirit came from the other realm. But with unfallen Adam, the soul was his center. Man's spirit was an *instrument* from the other realm. Adam's spirit was not his center, nor was it a life form.

Remember that Adam had a part left out. There was a biological part missing!* Adam had a human spirit that was made to contain something from the other realm.

As Jesus Himself so uniquely put it, flesh gives birth to flesh, and spirit gives birth to spirit. That is the *Genesis principle:* "After its kind." All creatures, including the descendants of Adam, are after their kind. (So also is this carpenter who came from two realms and is of both "kinds"!) What was missing in Adam that would have been "kind after its kind"? God had purposed that the *life* that was in the fruit of that wondrous Tree of Life was to be in Adam's spirit. As Adam's soul was the container of human life, so Adam's spirit was to contain the life from the fruit of the Tree of Life.

Adam had been invited to partake of the highest life, thereby becoming a visible son of the invisible God. *God would have had a species,* living on this planet, in the Garden of Eden, who were human yet had the life of God in their spirits . . . living by *His* life.

Adam never ate of that tree, so *he ended up being an unfinished creature!* Adam was biologically different from what God had designed him to be. He ended up with a part missing. An incomplete species. No wonder life has never really made sense to his race.

How did the Nazarene carpenter differ biologically from Adam? The answer is found in the difference between Adam's spirit and the Lord's! Deep within the Lord Jesus His *living* spirit *did* contain something! That is the difference between the two men!

---

* Remember that we are using the term *biological* to include the nonphysical life forms. See the chart on page 8.

Look very close! *Divine life* is there inside the carpenter's human spirit! *His* spirit contains the divine Spirit. The very life of God makes its abode within the spirit of Jesus Christ. In fact, the two are *one.* A life form is in His soul; it is human life. A life form is in His human spirit; it is *the* life. The highest life. Eternal life. *The* Spirit lives inside Jesus Christ. Your Lord has the highest life pulsating within Him.

Inside of Jesus Christ is something that was never inside Adam. There is *nothing* missing in the carpenter! No "parts" are left out. The fruit of the Tree of Life is inside this Galilean. In fact, He *is* the Tree of Life. He *is Life. He* is Eternal Life.

Jesus Christ is a life form. Which life form? He is the highest life form made visible!

The Lord declared that very fact: "I am life."

Paul declared it, "Christ, my *life."*

Now, let us see the answer to our key question. We have asked it of God, of angels, of Adam. When Jesus Christ, a carpenter living in Galilee, got out of bed in the morning, what life did He live by? He lived by means of the same life that God the Father lives by. Jesus Christ lived by a life not given to Him by Mary. He lived by a life not human. He lived by means of the highest life.

So we see the biological uniqueness of Jesus Christ. Unfallen Adam started out as (1) soul, (2) spirit, (3) body. Jesus Christ was (1) *spirit,* (2) soul, (3) body.

Jesus Christ was the *first* one ever to be *spirit,* then soul and body. *That* is the biological order God had planned for Adam. But this proper order never existed in man until Jesus Christ.

But more! Jesus Christ had a *normal* soul. When the soul is second, it is normal. The human soul is never totally normal until it is under the direction of that higher *life* residing within the spirit.

Jesus Christ was the first person ever to have a *truly* normal soul. The soul's emotions were there, but they never over-reached their natural boundaries. On the other hand, they were never unnaturally suppressed.

His soul's *will* was there, too. But He did not attempt to live the Christian life by the determination and grit of human will. His will was neither strong nor weak. It was in submission to a higher life.

But it was the normality of His *mind* that was in such contrast to the intellect, reasoning, and rationale of *all* those who were around Him.

His mind was incredibly normal. This may come as a shock to you, dear reader, but Jesus Christ was not a great intellectual. To have been so would have tilted Him far, far to the human side, leaving the divine side out of balance.

We always think that the intellect is superior. But the truth is, when it comes to rationalism, cognition, and out-and-out braininess, God is disconcertingly *simple.* Put it another way: Fallen human life is highly intellectual. That is the nature of man's *fallen* state.

Never forget: When the highest life form came to earth, He drove the third-highest life form a bit mad with His incredible simplicity. It is the third life form on the biological chart that ascends to the greatest heights of rationalism. Move in either direction on the biological chart, up or down, and you will find a form of life intellectually *less* complex than man!

The men who were the intellects of Jesus' day hit Him with the most complex, profound questions that the IQ of man could conjure up. He drove them mad with answers that spoke of birds, flowers, sunsets, wind, and water.

His mind's faculties were normal. His thoughts, His teachings, His life were simple and uncomplex. Both His words and His life-style dripped with a sense (1) of simplicity and (2) of things unseen. His *other* habitat, located in another realm, is not known for intellectualism and rationalism.

Today the *intellect* is always seen as superior to and trusted more than either *emotions* or *will*. Your Lord, the highest life, seemed to show great compassion and *patience* with emotional people (Peter, the woman at the well, the woman who spoke of crumbs that dropped from the table); He *tolerated* the willful (the rich young ruler); He had an out-and-out *disdain* toward the mindy ones (Pharisees, scribes, Sadducees). Not to mention a running war with them that culminated in His murder.

Perhaps this One who could roam the paths of history, both past and future, already knew what frontal-lobe people of the future would do to the Christian faith and to simple believers! What have they done? They have established that our faith is primarily intellectual understanding of doctrine. This concept has, of course, very little to do with living the Christian life *by means of a life within us.*

Pause for a moment and ask the question: If His species did begin to multiply, *and* if they *also* began to live by the higher life in them, what would these people eventually come to be like? Would they be

43

people first of the soul, or first of the spirit? Complex or simple? Mindy, emotional, strong-willed, or something totally different from all three of those? Rationalistic? Moralistic? Mostly of this realm, with values tied to tangible things? Or of the unseen, the intangible? Or would they be a people seeking experiential knowledge of God—fellowship with God?

What of Jesus' sinless body? Before He lifted off this planet for the last time, His body *changed*. His body had become a *spiritual* body. The term "spiritual body" is a contradiction in terms. *Spiritual* is of the unseen, invisible, and without mass or molecules. *Body* is of the seen, is physical, has mass and molecules.

For Jesus, the two realms from which He had come met, reconciled, and expressed themselves in His translated body.

What a species! His body was not, and is not, bound by space-time. Do you recall the story?

One Sunday night in Jerusalem that body penetrated physical matter, yet was visible. And today His body is visible, yet spiritual and divine. He is physical, yet He now lives in the spiritual realm in unapproachable light. He plans to return to this physical realm again. He will be visible, yet utterly glorified. What a species!

Later we will look at how all this affects you and your walk with the Lord Jesus. But for now, we must ask a question, the answer to which is crucial to your spiritual life: Just how did Jesus Christ go about living by a life not human? *How* did He live by the highest life? Let us pursue that question *now,* and for all the rest of our lives.

EIGHT

The Father as Life to Jesus Christ

If you want to know your Lord better, then you begin your quest by understanding what was going on in His life *internally* when He lived on earth. Ask Jesus Christ how *He* lived the Christian life. It is not Peter nor John nor Paul who can best show you how to lay hold of an indwelling Lord. Rather, it is He who was indwelt by His Father and who now indwells you who can best lead you to living by a life not your own!

I live by My Father.

How did Jesus Christ live by the life of the Father? How did He live by the highest life? What experience lay behind this incredible statement?

His answer will open a whole new vista of the spiritual walk for *your* Christian walk. We will look at His life in two parts: His experience on earth (1) before He began to minister, and (2) during His three-year ministry.

At first it would seem there is little or nothing you and I could know about Jesus' "spiritual life" before age thirty. But if we take a look at the things going on in His life at age thirty, we can assume He had acquired these attributes at some time in His life between His birth and age thirty. So let us consider the spiritual maturing of the Son of God.

Lying there in Mary's arms, the little baby did *not* look up and say, "I'm pretending to be a baby, but I am the Son of God come down from the heavenlies; I'll go on pretending to grow up for the next decade or so." He was a real baby, and He grew as any other child. As His body grew and matured, His soul grew and matured in lock step with His body. But unlike any other child, He had a living spirit. His awareness of this internal dimension also grew in lock step with the growth and maturity of His soul and body. He is the only person who ever was (or ever will be) born with a living spirit and an indwelling Father. (Adam had been created full grown. Besides, he had no indwelling Lord.)

What and how did He learn and grow spiritually? The question is fascinating. If you can gain even the slightest glimpses of the spiritual maturing of your Lord as He grew up, it could (1) revolutionize your understanding of the proper spiritual maturing of a believer and (2) open up whole new meanings to the words *spirit* and *spiritual*. After all, it was your Lord who more or less "invented" terms such as *spirit, spiritual,* and *heavenly places.* These are words to us;

they were *experiences* to Him. He used these words to describe *His* experience. *Your Lord's* experience in eternity past, His own personal experience in touching the spiritual realm as He grew up, His internal walk with His Father in His spirit during His three-year ministry—these experiences were what He conveyed through His words. He invented words to describe the reality of His divine fellowship with the Father and the Holy Spirit during those eras of His life.

All Christian experiences share their origin in *His* encounter with things spiritual. Learn His experience and you will discover the *how* of *your* walk with the Lord.

Words He used to describe His experiences come to us only as words. Those words need to be turned back into experience so that we can truly know what He spoke about.

Here is one thing He discovered as He grew up that would appear to be wholly outside our little acre of reality. He discovered that He could remember the past. You and I read John 1:1-5 and Colossians 1, and there discover He created everything. Well, there had to come a day in the life of the young apprentice to a carpenter when He made that same discovery about Himself. A moment came when He remembered the day *He* had created the spirituals and the physicals.

As early as age twelve, he knew who his Father was. On the night before his crucifixion he was—*at least* by that time—wholly one with his Father. It was the Father who said, "Have I been so long with you and you have not known me?" He dared to say, "Before Abraham was, I am." He spoke to the Father in this amazing dialogue.

Before the foundation of the world
you loved me!

He often spoke of *returning* to the heavenlies, where he had once lived! Somewhere along the pathways of growing up, He remembered having been in God back there in the eternals of the Godhead.

From this, we learn a great deal about His internal experience: His body did not reveal these things to Him. His soul did not reveal these things to Him. His spirit revealed to Him experiences He had had in eternity past as the eternal Son and as Creator.

Point: His spirit could remember past eternity. We have learned a little about the spiritual life of Jesus and one of the features of His internal being.

But more. He could also remember the past events of space-time. He spoke intently of personally *knowing* people who had lived long ago. They seemed to have met and known Him, too. (Example: the Transfiguration when He met with Moses and Elijah. They knew Him.)

But the implications are more dramatic than even this. It appears His spirit could not only see the past but could roam the past. How is that possible? His spirit is from the spiritual realm. In that realm, space, time, matter, mass, distance, dimensions, even past and future seem not to exist, at least not as we think of such things. The clock simply does not tick in the nonmaterial realm.

If this is true, then your God does roam the corridors of time. There is mystery in the fact that He is in our space-time universe *and* in the non-dimensional universe *at the same time.* He was from two realms, and it appears He could be in *both* of them at the same time.

Consider His words:

"Abraham *saw* My day" (John 8:56).

"The Son of Man who came down from the heavenlies and who is now in the heavenlies" (John 3:13).

He said to unbelievers, "Where I *go* you cannot come" (John 13:33).

He made it more mind-boggling as He declared, "Where I *am* you cannot come" (John 7:34, 36).

Your Lord had a place deep within Him that appears to have been unfettered by our material and dimensional universe.

Your Lord had a spirit that could recall past eternity and past human history. He could remember having been there!

Perhaps the most difficult thing for us poor creatures to realize, being so utterly captive here in our space-time continuum, is that He began to remember the *future!*

"They will see the Son of man coming on the clouds" (Matt. 26:64).

"I was watching Satan fall from heaven like lightning" (Luke 10:18).

"I am the Alpha and the Omega. Who is, who was, and who is to come" (Rev. 1:8).

"When He has been killed, He will rise three days later" (Mark 9:31).

Now how could anyone remember eternity future when it hasn't happened yet?

Well, who says it hasn't happened yet!

Of course, it has not happened yet, not down here in our little space-time village. But *we* cannot say eternity future has not happened for Him. After all, all things are *in* Him. Space, the physical realm, all mass, all time, and all time continuums are in Him. But add this: All the spiritual realm and all eternity are *in* Him.

With eternity in Him, He is at the front and back of the eternals—at the same time!

Here on this earth (far beyond our ability to understand), deep within the place of His spirit, He was free of all confines. There He became aware of *all* His past; He became aware of *all* His future. He laid hold of His pre-existence. He laid hold of that age *after* creation, His post-creation existence! He *knew* He would return to glory when He returned to the Father.

Somewhere in His maturing, He had discovered He could remember the *future.* He saw Himself being crucified and resurrected. He saw His ascension. He saw the destruction of Jerusalem. He saw His return to this planet in power and glory, with the elect angels. Much of this, or similar things, *must* have happened to Him before the age of thirty.

It seems that sometimes the past, present, and future passed before Him as timeless. He sometimes spoke of future things as having happened. For instance, he often spoke to His disciples as though the cross had already redeemed them and they had already received the Holy Spirit. To Him, these things were *already* done. From His viewpoint in the eternals, these men had already been redeemed and had received an indwelling Holy Spirit.

Somewhere along the way in growing up, He realized He could actually see spiritual, invisible events as they took place.

> I saw Satan
> like lightning,
> falling.

Exactly how this all came about, we simply do not know. But this we know: His Father lived in Him, and He became aware of that fact. At some point He began to hear His Father speak—from within.

We take for granted some of the Lord's amazing language, ascribing it, perhaps, to some prophetic gift. More likely the answer is to be found in the mysteries connected with the operation of His spirit.

We assume that while He was growing up He discovered He could see present things happening that were beyond the reach of His eyes. He knew people He had never met, knew what they were thinking, and even saw them. He said:

> Your child is healed.
> Those who betray me are coming even now.
> You will find a donkey there.
> Catch a fish, open its mouth . . .
> Lazarus is dead.
> Cast your nets on the other side.
> Zacchaeus, come down.
> So, you are Peter.
> I saw you, Nathanael, under the tree.
> You speak truthfully, you have had five husbands.
> One of you is a traitor.

Have I been so long with you and you have not
known me?

All of this indicates His human spirit can roam
eternity and is not always confined to knowing only
the things geographically nearby in the present.

Do believers sometimes have glimpses of this? If
so, why? Is such a marvelous thing for prophecy? For
miracles? To impress your friends? Absolutely not!
Rather, it is for fellowship with God . . . allowing you
to fellowship with Him in time and in the eternals.

Whatever the attributes of the human spirit may
be or may not be, this one fact is certain: The human
spirit is there so that we might have fellowship with
the Living God.

Your Lord's spirit—one with the Father, who is
Spirit—was unfettered and unaffected by our space-
time universe, even as He lived in it. While standing
on the soil of this planet, He was free to dwell outside
the fences of height, depth, breadth, and the ticks of
time. Living in this physical creation, He was not at
all bound by its boundaries. He could see even *beyond*
the last moments of space-time and behold events
that were beyond all endings into the ineffable places
of a future where there is *only* the eternals.

Dear reader, I pause here to remind you that this
book is not about prophecy, or miracles, or signs, or
wonders. This book is about fellowship with your
Lord, *now*. And about the fact that *spirit* is a much
higher word than it has been given credit for, as it
relates to your walk with Jesus Christ. And so is *life*.

There was also a day in the life of this incredible
young carpenter when He began to hear voices!

Voices?

Yes, voices. Or more correctly, a voice. Not a voice out in front of Him. Nor behind Him. Not *anywhere* outside of Him. Nor was that voice in the hearing of His ears. That voice spoke to Him *deep* in His spirit.

He heard His Father speaking. His Father was *in* Him. Right there in that limitless, immeasurable, nondimensional spirit, *there,* the Living God dwelt! *In* Him! Again, this indwelling is not about power or prophecy. That was not the purpose of the indwelling Spirit for Him, nor for you. An indwelling Father and an indwelling voice meant one thing to Jesus Christ *above all else:* the privilege of fellowship. First and foremost, fellowship with His Father.

Imagine that day when He first uttered, in the astonishment of the most staggering of all revelations:

I and My Father
are One!

Remember, this book is about walking with the Lord Jesus Christ. Here He is found walking with His Father and living by means of His life—one with His Father.

It was not authority, nor power, nor miracles that awed your Lord. The holiest thing in the universe to Him was that His Father lived inside of Him and that He inseparably shared one single *life* with His Father.

Here is another attribute of His no one else on earth had: Whenever He met someone, He could tell whether or not that person was dead or alive. He could tell if one day they would be recipients of eternal life or if they were just dead men, walking.

Was this something He sensed within, or did He journey back to that primordial era before the foundation of the world when He chose (predestined) those very ones who would receive eternal life?

The purpose of this glimpse at the childhood and early manhood experiences of the Lord Jesus Christ is to contrast Him with fallen man. They really are two biologically *different* species. Fallen man was not only different from Jesus because of man's corrupted flesh, damaged soul, and inoperative spirit, as over against the Lord's sinless body, perfect soul, and living spirit. There was more to it than that. The Lord Jesus had parts in Him, functioning parts, that fallen man *never* had! All his faculties were flawless, *plus* He had a higher life in Him. And He lived by that life. And in so doing, He experienced a way of living on this earth that no other creature had ever known before.

This is a subject that has been largely overlooked, yet it is a focus that is vital to you and to me as believers. After all, you have been *regenerated* (that is, your spirit has been "re-*livened*"). You have things going on inside of you that are not in the unbeliever. You have a resurrected spirit. The unbeliever does not. You have a cleansed soul. The unbeliever does not. Your soul also exists in the presence of a resurrected spirit and that fact is influencing—even transforming—your soul. The unbeliever has no such wonder going on in him. What about the physical body of the believer and unbeliever? There is good news here. You have the hope of a new, glorified body. The unbeliever does not. Your spirit has also been made one with God's spirit, *and* God's life—the highest life—is in your spirit!

There is another and higher form of life that is now dwelling in you. You are *soul*, but you also *have* a spirit. Even more, these are two life forms in you, and when you get out of bed in the morning, you have the opportunity of laying hold of that other life.

Today *spirit* and *Holy Spirit* are very popular terms, but perhaps for the wrong reason. To many, those words conjure up thoughts of success, happiness, power, prophecies, wonders, casting out demons, and other such spectaculars. But those words on the lips of Jesus Christ mean something else.

What did it mean for Jesus to be able to get up in the morning and live by the highest life that indwelt Him? Power? Success? Being happy? What was the highest, most sacred thing to Jesus Christ about having His very own Father indwelling Him?

The answer is simple, incredibly simple. Life-changing in its simplicity. The thing that meant the most to Jesus Christ was having His Father indwelling him, there in the realm of the *spirituals.* The thing that throbbed within His inmost being was that He could have *fellowship*—fellowship with His Father!

That was supreme above all else. The Lord Jesus had been part of the Godhead throughout all eternity past. There within the *fellowship* of the Godhead, your Lord had fellowshiped with His Father for a long, long time! How long? For all eternity past, that's how long! *This* He cherished above all else. To come to this planet and continue that fellowship right here on earth meant so much more to Him that miracles, signs, success, power, etc., were insignificant by comparison.

You, a redeemed child of God, have been given a spiritual nature through your salvation. People in your lifetime will tell you all about the spirit and the Holy Spirit and dazzle you with tales of power, ordering demons around, having visions, prophecies, predictions, miracles. "Successful Christian living"! These all seem shallow when compared with your Lord's placing fellowship with His Father above all else. "The deeper Christian life" is what the Lord Jesus had in His continuing fellowship with the Father.

"Spirit" and "life" were concepts He had known as His own experience long before creation, long before dreams, healing, miracles, or success ever existed. As the Lord reflected back to His pre-existence in eternity within the Godhead, such words meant one thing to Him: the fellowship of the Godhead!

And on earth, His spirit made possible one thing above all else: His spirit allowed Him to continue a fellowship with the Father that had begun in and belonged to eternity. His spirit allowed that fellowship to continue here on this planet. That experience of fellowship in the Godhead was cherished by Him above all else.*

Throughout the last 1,700 years, an intimate fellowship with the Lord *within* the believer's spirit has been relegated to the back row. And to the footnotes. It is well past due for rediscovery.

---

* A remarkable species, wouldn't you say? Too bad this one-of-a-kind species suffered extinction after only thirty-three years upon this planet. What a race of people that would have been. On the other hand, there were rumors He didn't stay dead. Maybe that species has not suffered extinction after all.

Why did it so completely disappear? The answer is not known to me. Perhaps it is because we talk about that which we know the best and hold in suspicion that which we know the least. Perhaps it is because surface things are more easily grasped. Perhaps the *how* of a deeper walk with Christ has simply been lost to the family of God's people.

If you, the seeker, ask *how* to know your Lord better, more intently, and more deeply, you might get a quick answer such as, "Read your Bible more and pray more." If you *have* reached the point of *asking* this question, however, the chances are you already have a shelf full of worn-out Bibles and very calloused knees, and are looking for something that is *beyond* prayer and Bible study.

One thing is fairly certain. You will often receive blank stares from even the most revered of Christian leaders if you should ask, "How do I set up lines of communication with an indwelling Lord?" "Tell me something about how to live by the life that Jesus Christ lived by." And you might be wise to skip entirely, "How do I enter into the fellowship that is going on within the Godhead?"

May the day come when these matters are the primary pursuit of not just the individual Christian but of the entire ecclesia itself. We have no higher calling than to pursue that which Jesus Christ pursued while He sojourned on this planet . . . to know, walk in, walk with, enter into fellowship with an indwelling Lord.

In the meantime, remember that His human spirit can travel all of space and time and all of eternity, can contain the life of His Father, can hear

His Father speak, can allow Him to fellowship with His Father, is one with His Father, and is in the place where the Father's life and the Son's life are one. Furthermore, in all the many-faceted elements of this spiritual place, fellowship with His Father ranks above all else. If his species were to multiply on this earth, is it possible they might also touch this same spiritual world within them, and for the same purpose, that is, knowing their Lord?

In the next chapter, we will continue pursuing this very matter: your Lord's relationship to the realm within Him.

NINE

Two Species Contrasted

Three incomparable years! A *man* on this planet living by a life higher than human life!

You are very familiar with the three years of the Lord's ministry. But let's take a look at those years from a new vantage point. Let's look at them from a *biological* view. Doing so is almost like a rediscovery of those years.

How did a man who had both the highest life and the third-highest life in Him differ from the inhabitants of this planet, who had only Adam's fallen life in them and had only fallen human life to live by?

To help answer that, consider the difference between an eel and an *electric* eel. The electric eel looks just like an ordinary eel except he has *organs* operating in him that are utterly unknown to the ordinary eel.

Jesus Christ and fallen man were even more different than that. If His species multiplied, His offspring would be different too.

Look also at a radio transmitter and a receiver. But not a radio that picks up signals locally, nor even from way out in deep space. Imagine a radio transmitter that can send and receive signals to *another* dimension. Mind you, not just to some distant place light years away, but to another creation not in this space-time continuum.

Jesus Christ had something in Him that could do just that. (If His species multiplied, so could *his offspring,* at least to some degree.)

Now consider a human and a bat. When you walk into a room, how do you *perceive* that room? Height, depth, color, smell, furnishing, arrangement. And a bat? Being virtually blind, it perceives that same room in a totally different way. It perceives the room by listening to echoes of sounds that it sends out. Obviously, to the bat the room is something totally different from what man considers the room to be.

When your internal parts are so different from a bat's, the two of you perceive this world totally differently. So also Jesus Christ and fallen man, for their internal parts differed.

An electric eel is different from other eels because of specialized parts within it. A radio device that sets up communications with another universe is unlike an ordinary radio transmitter. In the same way, two different species come out with totally different perceptions of their surroundings. Why? Because of their biological makeup.

Jesus Christ apprehended His surroundings differently than fallen man did.

Let us turn from the biological to the sociological. Here the differences between the highest life on the biological chart and that of the third-highest life form become astounding.

Mores. The contrast between these two species on their views of morals is staggering. The religious leaders of fallen *Homo sapiens* had *high morals* (especially for everyone *except* themselves). Though they had some sins of their own, they were ready to stone to death an adulterous woman, on the spot. But the One who was the "religious leader" of the other universe (and was Himself utterly without sin) was more than willing to let her go scot-free.

It was not the religious leaders of *this* planet whose companions were prostitutes and thieves. It was the One who had lived in the unapproachable light of *holiness* who ran around with the "lowlife" of society. Your Lord was a liberal when it came to morals. Not for Himself, but for *us!* His expectations of our moral conduct were, to say the least, *very realistic.*

It was not a religious leader of our planet who enjoyed *fellowship* so much that he left the impression he ate too much and drank too much. No, it was the Lord of the heavenlies; He was labeled a drunk and glutton! (The conduct of the *highest* life, mind you, got this label.) The man with God in Him had that reputation. This one *really* enjoyed fellowship! What a reputation to be placed on the greatest "religious" leader of all time . . . and all eternity.

Culture. Have you ever considered the *cultural* differences between those of us who gained our culture from customs here on earth and One whose culture was instilled in Him through endless ages while living in the very center of God?

The differences between cultures here on earth are dramatic enough. Americans are taught to keep one hand in the lap while eating; in Europe, that is out-and-out vulgarity. An Italian is constantly touching another Italian while talking; an Englishman *never* touches another Englishman!

Earth's many, many cultures place high premiums on cultural expression. Our cultures show up in religious rituals, special places of worship, courtship, marriage, sports and recreation, social rituals, dress and fashion, and social amenities. But the life of the Godhead exchanges all of that for one thing: fellowship!

Values. Nowhere is the biological chasm between fallen third-class life more clearly contrasted with the highest form of life than in their different *value systems!*

A pretty good way to anticipate what the values of "life form number one" might be is to expect that, whatever it is, it will be the *opposite* of our value system.

We hold to *gaining;* He valued *losing.* We cherish life; He placed higher value on death, especially death to *self.* We stand in awe of the rich and riches; He valued the poor and looked askance at the rich. We acquire; He encouraged giving up all. We value the "seen" as best of all; He valued the "unseen" and counted precious little in the visible creation to be of any real worth. The visible creation was, after all, so temporal; the other one was permanent. That which was "above" was everything to Him; everything "here" is of the highest value to fallen *Homo sapiens.*

Suffering was crucial to His set of values; fallen man values escape from suffering as wise, at any cost. Such, for fallen man, is simply evidence of sanity.

And just how could people here *see* the other realm? He stated that there was only one way. He established that as an absolute. You had to be born in that other realm in order to see that realm (John 3:3). He declared He was from that realm. He said that His realm was "above" and that His followers would all be born in that place. Above! His followers would actually be born *in* that other realm.

"Above" was obviously a special and wonderful place to Him.*

The spirits of fallen (third-class) life were filled with death. But His spirit was alive and filled with the divinity of the Father and the Holy Spirit (Luke 4:1).

Jesus was *led* by His spirit. That is quite different from the rather unreliable instruments (the mind, emotions, and will) by which the fallen species was led.

It is at this point that the difference between the *thinking* of fallen man and the "thinking" of Jesus provides us with the greatest contrast between the values of third-class life and the highest life. They *thought.* He did something higher than *thinking.* His

---

* John 3:3, 31; 8:23; 19:11. John 3:3 is correctly translated "born from above," *not* "born again."

way of *apprehending* His surroundings was not by means of "thinking instruments." Remember, He had a different internal makeup and operated on some other plane than did man with his instrumentations.

> Jesus did not
> trust Himself to them.
> For He knew
> what was *in* man.
> (John 2:24)

This higher life in Jesus put Him light years above fallen man in "apprehending His surroundings."

Just see the biological difference between these two species as they clash over a *healing incident.* Contrast their internal differences as revealed in the healing of the paralytic.

> They (fallen man) began to *reason* in their *hearts.*
> Jesus, *perceiving* in His *spirit*
> that they *reasoned,* said,
> "Why do you *think* evil?"
> (Matt. 9:2-8; Mark 2:1-12; Luke 5:17-26)

Pharisees, scribes, and law teachers—very definitely *not* believers—were listening to Jesus in the town of Capernaum. Some persistent men let a cripple down through the roof. Jesus *saw* their faith. (Who can "see" faith?) The Pharisees, scribes, and teachers could only "reason" in their hearts at the unfolding scene. Their "reason" concluded Jesus had blasphemed.

The Lord was equipped with *more* than the faculty to reason. Jesus sensed their logic. That is, he

had a "spiritual knowing" of their rationalized con-
clusions. They reasoned in mind. He *perceived in his
spirit!* These are two totally different places. He did
not reason in his mind but perceived in his spirit!

His response to them: "You *think* evil."

This scene gives a perfect glance at one endowed
with "parts" from another realm (a living spirit; the
life and Spirit of God) as over against fallen men
whose fallen mental logic was their highest and best
equipment for understanding spiritual things.

They thought. His species did something higher
than that. In this incident He employed not His soul
life, but His higher life. And *there* within the realm of
the functionings of His higher life He did not *think,
he perceived. Where* did He perceive? *In* His spirit!

Fallen man, with soul operating at full capacity,
reasons, intellectualizes, "logics," and thinks. Fallen
man does all this from out of the seat of his fallen
human life, that is, from out of his damaged soul.
This is why we sometimes say the fallen soul "mutated." The soul became other than what it was supposed to be, amplifying portions out of their natural
area of intended functions.

It is difficult for us to describe what He did. In
contrast to *reasoning,* He had a *"knowing."* He did not
intellectualize; He "revelated" (apprehended by revelation, something taking place not in His mind but in
His spirit). Instead of thinking, rationalizing, and
using dialectics, your Lord did something wholly different from that! He *intuited!*

Of course, He completely outclassed the other life
form when it came to a discussion. How? By simply
listening to a voice coming from the other realm.

That is, a voice from within His spirit. That voice was His Father's. And what he heard and repeated, coming from His Father and spoken to fallen man, dumbfounded their every question and stupefied their every observation.

Poor souls, they did not know they were dealing with a higher life form. (After all, He looked like all the rest of them.) Unaware of His biological uniqueness or that He was *two* life forms higher up on the biological chart than they, it is no wonder He appeared quite mad to His enemies.

They used the instrumentation of this planet: They thought. He used instrumentation of another realm and another life form: He perceived.*

We will close this chapter by turning to a question that begs for an answer. When they killed Him, did that end this one-of-a-kind species?

Quite the opposite. When they killed Him, it ended *their* species!

He crucified that old and fallen species. From His view, the fallen race of the fallen sons of a fallen Adam is now *extinct!*

That poor species was hopeless and beyond all help, so He just did away with it! He started over again with a new species and a brand-new creation. In killing Him, they brought total extinction to their entire biological life form; and He, after His resurrection, launched a new species . . . after *His* kind.

Is there hope that this wonderful new species (Jesus Christ), this wonderful new form of life (Jesus Christ), this wonderful *higher* life (Jesus Christ) . . .

---

* See addenda I and II for other examples of the differences between the highest life and the third-highest life.

that it might multiply? Any chance He might have some younger *brothers* and *sisters?* Would this biologically unique species begin to populate this planet?

If you could become one who belonged to His species, if you had a higher life implanted in you, if *you* could live by the highest life, if *you* could live by the same life that Jesus Christ lived by, and if that life matured in you, *then* you could expect at least *some* of what has been seen in these last two chapters to become part of *your* experience!

An implantation of a spiritual element on a spiritual plane. That is what would be necessary.

Did His species suffer extinction on the cross? On the contrary. Something else was discovered about His particular life form that weekend.

> It was discovered that Jesus Christ could (and He is the *only species* who can) pass *His* life form on to another life form. He could even pass His highest life on to a *lower* life form!

Furthermore, this risen Jesus could give His life form to these creatures, not in small quantities but in a great abundance. Not a little of this highest life. No! He could give His life and the life of His Father to these creatures in *incredible measure* (John 10:10). And as His Father lived by means of that *life,* and as He had lived by means of *that* life, so they would also live by that life. Here may just be the most incredible promise ever made.

> As I have lived by My Father,
> Even so shall you live by Me!
> (John 6:57)

Who were these fortunate people? And did they really have this highest life placed in them? Did they *really* have two life forms in them? Did they really have the opportunity to live by the highest life when they got out of bed every morning? When this new species got out of bed in the morning, could they really live by a life not their own? Could they really, truly, *actually* live by the same life that Jesus Christ lived by when He got out of bed in the morning?

Well, let's meet *one* such man. In fact, let us meet the first person who had been a member of Adam's old and fallen race and also became the first to ever experience the resurrection of his spirit and who . . . oh, let me stop there, for we surely do not want to spoil *this* story.

TEN

Simon Peter

The scene: a room somewhere in Jerusalem. The time: Sunday night.

This morning Jesus Christ had risen from the dead. (At least all evidence points in that direction.) But of those assembled in that room, *none* is ready to believe it. Every door and window is locked. Fear prevails.

Not a likely setting for the greatest event in human history, is it? What is about to happen in that room has had no comparison since Adam *almost* ate of the Tree of Life.

Jesus Christ appears. Out of nowhere. Consternation, terror, and confusion reign.

After a few minutes, the people *begin* to settle down. It really is He. But just who is *He?* A lot has happened in three days. And just what is His relationship to these people now?

First, the Man standing there is not just resurrected. He *is Resurrection.* Consequently, *He* can raise things from the dead! Even things dead so long that their death had taken place during Adam's lifetime.

The One standing there is also Life. *The* Life. He is also a species. A one-of-a-kind species. Nothing else like Him exists in either realm.

He is a life form. He *is* Life itself. He is the *highest* life. But more. By some mystery of His death and resurrection, He is able to give His unique life form to anyone whom His Father chooses.

And the Father has chosen.

Whom?

The people in that locked room. And so the plot thickens!

A lone grain of wheat had fallen into the ground three days before, had died there, and then had come up as the highest life. But that one seed of divine life is now *many.* And that "many seed" can be planted inside other people!

Watch closely what happens to these people. What happened to them just may have also happened to you. (The only difference? None really. Except maybe this: No one has ever told *you* this has happened to you!)

Earlier that day this lone species had called His followers *brothers.* That is not possible, of course. These men simply were not *genetically* kin to Him. Their "genes" were all of the earth. They had no "genetics" on a spiritual plane. They had not yet received the life of His species. How could He call them "brothers" who had not received His life? They had a lower life form, of earth. He had the highest life, and it was a form of life that belonged totally to another realm.

But try to remember: He is One who is free of the limits of our space-time continuum. He speaks of future things as having already happened—especially things that are just about to happen any moment now. And sure enough, it really happened. Right there, right then, a transfer of heavenly "genetics" to earthly people.

The Lord Jesus walked over to Simon Peter. He looked at Peter. Then He looked inside of Simon Peter!

What was there, *inside?* The same thing that was in all the sons of fallen Adam. Simon Peter had a body that had become flesh, indwelt by sin. Condition: hopeless.

Deeper within: a greatly damaged soul (as anyone who knew Peter could testify). Look at his soul. Peter's *emotions* often got the best of him. As to his *will*, he boasted of having a strong will, but he was really very weak in this area. As to his *mind,* well, this illiterate was *anything* but an intellect; but he had an opinion about everything. And he was usually wrong—typical soul! Most of all, Peter's soul had sinned; it was scarlet, desperately in need of cleansing.

But even deeper. There in Peter's *inmost* being lay the greatest tragedy of his life. Peter's spirit lay dead within him. Only the power to resurrect the dead could help a spirit that was otherwise eternally doomed to be cut off from the realm from which it had come.

A resurrection that could bring something back to life *forever?* Unbelievable! And raising something from the dead that does not even belong to this universe was *beyond* preposterous.

But watch.

As you know, the creating God had not breathed into the nostrils of a man since that moment long ago, in the garden, when He had created this particular species. Well, that very God is back. He is about to inaugurate a whole *new* creation! But this time He is not only *Creator,* He is Lord over Death! What is more, tonight He will *not* create. This time, in this room, He will do more than create. He will gain a new title: LIFEGIVER. What He will do has nothing to do with creation—at least not the old concept of a creation. He is about to give Peter something *uncreated.* There is only one thing that is uncreated: *God's own life!*

Standing before Lifegiver is one of the worst examples of a fallen man. A cursing, swearing, ignorant, capricious, unstable, God-denying, Lord-betraying, illiterate *fisherman.* One Simon Peter!

An unlikely specimen for launching a whole *new creation.* A poor candidate for becoming the first to become a brand-new species. The last time the Creator started a brand-new creation, He had started by creating the heavenlies and the earth. This time He would start a brand-new creation with . . . Simon Peter? A fear-stricken fisherman? Unbelievable!

Yes! And that should be a very wonderful encouragement to you!

Just three days ago, hanging on a tree, your Lord had destroyed the entire *first* creation. On the cross. The old humanity, the old civilization of man, the old earth, the old species, the law, all ordinances, all powers, all governments.

Annihilated!

Not to mention also sin *and* death!

Annihilated!

Your Lord took all those things into Himself and then carried them to the grave. From *His* viewpoint that whole creation, which He had created in six days, *no longer existed. Annihilated.* From His viewpoint the first creation had returned to its origin, to nothingness.

You might say God begins here to make a second creation (actually a new creation). This new creation is made out of that which is uncreated! It is made up of ingredients that existed before creation. He will use *His* life, the highest life, *un*created life, as the building blocks of His new creation.

His triumphant, resurrected life will be the first element used to build this new universe. Your Lord is out to launch a higher, better, greater, more glorious creation than the old. And do not question that this new creation is exactly *that.* Why? Because He used His own divinity as the ingredients for this new endeavor. And this is as high and glorious as things can get!

The first citizen of this new creation: An angel? A king? A governor? A planet? A galaxy? No. A bedraggled, dumbfounded, awestruck blue-collar worker from an ignominious borough called Galilee.

Stand by. There may yet be hope for you. And me.

The One who created all things now draws His breath. Is He about to create again? No. He becomes Lifegiver. The Lord of heaven and earth blows His very own lifegiving breath *into* a wide-eyed Simon Peter. Within that breath is not the wind of heaven, but the highest life itself. His Spirit! His life! His nature . . . now entering Peter!

Watch as *the* resurrected life slips into this man. See a new species being born. Behold the very first moments of a new creation. Simon Peter, of all people, the very first fruit of a new, and an eternal, creation.

The redemptive power of that life flows deep down into Peter's *soul*. Suddenly the soul is cleansed—cleansed from all sin. Made whiter than snow. The *first* step in a lifelong process to normalize Peter's soulical nature has begun.*

But deeper yet flows the highest life. Down into the very recesses of Peter's inmost being. As the living Spirit begins to approach the vicinity of Peter's long-dead spirit, that lifeless spirit *stirs.* An element of *resurrection life* touches that dead element in Peter that belongs to the spiritual realm. The divine Spirit, the highest life, touches the human spirit that has so long been coffered deep inside Peter's soul. *Life* touches Peter's spirit. For the first time in history, the dead spirit of a man rises from the dead.

Simon Peter has something alive somewhere down there inside him that was never alive before. Do you remember the origin of his spirit? Peter's

---

* You may not be familiar with the word *soulical.* Genesis tells us that man became a living soul at the point of his creation. His character is *soulical.* But fallen man came to have certain negative conduct, the source of which is his fallen soul. Paul refers to this as the *soulish* aspects of a natural, *un*spiritual man. Soulical, *psychikon,* as over against soulish, *psychikos.* Kenneth Wuest translates *psychikon* as "soulical" in I Corinthians 15: "Since there is a soulical body, there is also a spiritual body" (see I Cor. 15:44-46 in *The New Testament: An Expanded Translation*).

spirit originated in another universe. His spirit, which came from another realm, is now alive. Forever! Nothing, absolutely nothing, can ever kill this man's spirit again. Not death. Not hell. Not sin. Not Satan. Not all the powers of darkness. His *spirit* is beyond their reach. Nothing dies twice. The spirit, which belongs to this fisherman, is beyond reach of anything except eternal life.

For sure, there is a part of Simon Peter that is alive forever and will *never* again taste death!

But that is not all! The best is just about to happen.

The highest life, the nature of God, *the* Life, continues on its *inward* journey. Not content to just touch and resurrect Peter's spirit, the highest life now enters *into* Peter's spirit. Behold, the fruit of the Tree of Life *in a man!* Peter is about to become the first human being ever to partake of the Tree of Life.

> He who eats My flesh
> and
> drinks My blood.
> But I speak to you of
> My life and My Spirit,
> He who eats Me
> shall *live by* Me!
> As I live by the Father,
> so
> he who eats Me
> shall live by Me.
> I am the vine! *The* tree!

Something happened to Peter that had never happened to Adam. Peter partook of the proper *tree!*

The highest life, the nature of God, was coming into this man's living spirit. Furthermore, this life was at that very instant making *its home* in that man's spirit.

Even more.

This newly resurrected spirit belonging to Peter and *the* Spirit now joined and became *one*.

Far beyond anything your Lord did when He blew into Adam, the Lord Jesus blew His very *own life* into a fisherman. Simon Peter was the first mortal man to ever have *two* forms of life in him. Peter had just moved up the biological chart! He had just bade good-bye to the third place on the biological chart. He now had the highest life in him.

It would be a long, slow, unsteady start for Peter. Though conscious of *all* that had happened, *growth* in what had happened to Peter would take up the rest of his lifetime. Nonetheless, tomorrow morning, when Simon Peter got out of bed, he had a chance, yes, maybe only a small chance, but for the first time an ordinary human being had a *chance* to get out of bed and live by a life not his own. He had the possibility of

Living by the Highest Life.

Never before had any mortal man had such a possibility. Nor had two biologically different life forms ever before been inside a mere *mortal* at the same time.

Please note that Peter is a very slow learner. But little by little, he will discover the awesomeness of what has happened to him, and he *will* perceive all that is going on inside of him.

Right now, our fisherman is "nigh-on" speechless. He senses, with a sensing he has never before owned, that his soul has been forgiven, cleansed, and made holy. Also, he senses some vast awakening within him toward the spiritual sphere. He looks inside himself, trying to see what is going on. He searches for some audible expression. Wide-eyed, he stumbles for words. Finally, Peter stammers out a statement no man had ever before made:

> I . . . I . . . have become
> a partaker
> of the divine nature!
> (2 Pet. 1:4)

Peter, you have become the first fruit of a *new humanity.* You are now biologically different from fallen man—you partake of a higher life. You differ from the old race of men. You are something brand-new! You belong to a new species.

You have a new citizenship. In a new nation. A *new realm* of creation has just come into being. You have a new family. In fact, everyone in that room has a new civilization to explore on earth. And a new realm "out there" somewhere to explore.

Where? *Above,* that's where! And they have a new house to live in, the household of God (2 Pet. 3:13)!

From this day on, our first citizen of this new creation will be looking around for a new heaven and a new earth where he and the rest of his species can fit in. Simon Peter is realizing that he, a new creation, is going to need a new habitat! That new habitat *will* be found. And that habitat *will* fit this new species just perfectly.

Peter launched out into new dimensions that night. He continued growing in grace. He grew in experiencing His Lord. But the amazing thing is this: Long, long after the Lord ascended, Simon Peter was *still* getting to know his Lord, better and better, inside. How is that possible? Because their relationship to one another had moved *inside* Simon Peter (2 Pet. 3:18).

Is Peter's *soul* totally transformed? No. But the *life* dwelling in Peter's spirit is reaching out and *gradually* changing Peter's soul. The Spirit is slowly transforming his soul from glory to glory until one day, out there somewhere after the Lord leaves heaven to return again to earth, the line between the glorified spirit and the glorified soul will blur.

By Peter's internal fellowship with Christ, and by the work of the cross in Peter's soul, this fisherman will begin to experience the gradual transformation of his soul. Yes, it really will be a *lifelong* project.

And Peter's body? What of that hopeless tent he lives in? If it is hopeless, then where is hope? The answer is a mystery almost unfathomable. Nonetheless, there is hope.

I must confess, dear reader, I do not know how it is that God shall give us new bodies (or is it *"change* our old bodies"?). What follows in the next paragraph *seems* to me to be what will take place.

It would appear that Simon Peter received the *seed* of a glorified body at the same time he received the highest life! The problem is, he can't see it, nor use it, nor locate it. Not yet. It is an infinitely small seed. Small beyond all comprehension. If we are understanding correctly, that seed is down there, somewhere, in the inmost recesses of Peter's spiritual being. Waiting. Waiting for a *sound*. A sound? Yes! The sound of a *trumpet*.

The sound of a very special trumpet will cause that tattered old *outward* tent to dissolve and will call forth that hidden seed. That seed will burst forth in full glory. A resurrected, glorified, eternal body to match a soul that has been transformed into a spiritual entity. That body will come forth. It will be a body glorious, out from which will shine forth a living spirit in full bloom! A spirit radiating out through a spiritual soul and a spiritual body—that is Peter's destiny.*

Peter will begin speaking about "life." He will talk about the spirit and the spiritual realm, about living by another life. The words *spirit* and *life* will drop from his lips as often as they did from the Lord's. Later will come a man named Paul who will use the same words, and in the same way. These men were not speaking of teachings nor of theology. What had been experiential reality to Jesus Christ had become experiential reality to them. They used these words to explain their experience. These men lived by a life not their own. Dear reader, read their words. Having

---

* Why have we heard so little about the Lord's life in us, an indwelling Spirit and an indwelling Lord, and the Lord giving us His own life to live by? Why is spirit-soul-body virtually never mentioned? Why do men teach that we are only body and soul?

Because the ancient heathen philosophers taught that man was a body and a soul, and in the era following Constantine (A.D. 323) many pagan philosophers became Christians, the pagan idea of body and soul engulfed Christian thinking with the birth of so-called Christian philosophy. The idea that man is body and soul is so ingrained in Western thinking that it will probably forever remain the law and gospel in the higher circles of academia. And the Christian faith will ever suffer because of this error.

You might wish to read the whole story of this little-known aspect of Christian theology found in addenda III and IV in this book. There you will discover exactly why you rarely hear of man as anything except body and soul.

an indwelling Lord, fellowshiping with the Lord who dwells within you, living by a life not your own is yours to have in experience as much as it was for Peter, for Paul, and all the other believers who laid hold of this reality.

Thank you, Peter, for showing us just how incredible a thing happens to an ordinary person (just like us) when receiving *full* salvation. If all this can happen to you, Simon Peter, then it can take place in anyone. Move over, brother, because here come the rest of us! If you have the right to live by the highest life, so do we!

PART 3

And if these things be true, just how accurate are the things that have been taught us about what we must do to live the Christian life?

To have a deeper, more meaningful walk with the Lord Jesus, there is much to be unlearned. The next few chapters are to help you unlearn many things that very definitely need to be unlearned.

Perhaps you can identify with the new Christian who was glorying in his ignorance, "Boy was I lucky! I knew so little about the Christian life. I never learned how to do it the wrong way."

May his tribe increase.

ELEVEN

You and the Horseless Carriage

If you are a believer, then you do have divine life in you, dear reader. Did anyone ever tell you that? Did anyone ever tell you that when you were redeemed by your Lord, on that *very* day the life of God (the Father of our Lord Jesus) came to dwell in you? Did anyone, in *all* that you have been hearing about the Christian life all these years, happen to mention such a thing to you, even in passing?

If not, you are similar to most of us. And you are not much different from the old gentleman who stopped in at a carriage shop to buy a new buggy. The enthusiastic salesman introduced him to something he had never heard of . . . a *horseless* carriage. The salesman's enthusiasm awed him. "This carriage has beauty, it has class, comfort, style, and status," he

was told. The old gentleman was absolutely be-
dazzled and, therefore, bought that incredible horseless carriage. He then proceeded to have it hauled
home while he sat proudly in its beautiful leather-
covered seat. In fact, each day he went out and sat in
his beautiful horseless carriage, proud as a peacock
of his modern, new-fangled buggy. True, the carriage
never moved. Neither did the old man. But ah, its
beauty! And all those wonderful features!

The problem is obvious. The salesman neglected
to tell the old gentleman that this terribly beautiful,
absolutely wonderful, indescribably comfortable, utterly fashionable carriage *had a motor* inside. Not
knowing the carriage had this motor, the old gentleman had absolutely no avenue open to him to
allow the engine of that wondrous carriage to carry
him about.

There goes the old gentleman now. See him? That
is him over there. Yes, the old gentleman right over
there, the one *pulling* that carriage.

Why, pray tell, *why* did the salesman not tell the
old gentleman about the engine? Why let the old man
pull that buggy around all by himself? Is it because
the salesman himself did not know about the engine?
Or if he did, perhaps even the salesman did not grasp
its significance?

You have been sold on the comfort, convenience,
success, status, distinct advantages, investment op-
portunities, and futuristic potential of *the Christian
life.* (That is, all those things are yours if you work
very hard at it.) But, dear reader, they forgot to tell
you the Christian life comes with its own engine. *You*
are not supposed to be dragging the Christian life

around all on your own power. Laying aside the fact that you look utterly ridiculous (and the fact you have become an utter failure at being a horse), the truth lies here: You simply cannot live the Christian life.

You are neither a horse nor are you an internal-combustion engine.

You do not have to pull that thing around anymore. You do not make that carriage go—certainly not by forever pulling on its front bumper. You look a sight! Lay it all down. Explore a bit. *There is a switch around here somewhere.*

Jesus Christ lives the Christian life. I don't. You don't, and you can't. *He* does!

Wake up, dear reader. You have the highest life form in *you!*

This may all be new to you, but it is true nonetheless. If it is news to you, remember that it is very *good news.* True, most of us have never heard of such a thing. Or we did not hear it when it was said. Or we did not know we heard it when we did hear it. Or we did not know what it meant when we heard it. And did not know how important it was when we finally did hear it. And *right now* do not have the foggiest notion what to do with what we have heard, when finally we discover how important it is!

But there is one thing you can do, *right now.* Wipe the sweat off your brow and let go of that bumper!

TWELVE

The Little Ol' Lady Who Would Be an Angel

It was eleven o'clock on Sunday morning, and Pastor Trut was speaking on the subject "We Must Be Angels." The message was part of a series of sermons entitled, "How to Please God."

He cleared his throat, took an expansive sweep of his audience, and began.

> You are an angel. And because you are an angel, always remember that much is required of you.
>
> First of all, you must always be invisible. Always. Never forget that.
>
> Second, your task is to deliver messages. Messages *from* God to His creation.

Pastor Trut leaned over the pulpit, his face grave as he intoned:

Remember! God is depending on you. On *you!* To get those messages through. Never fail Him. It will break His heart and cause Him deep pain to see you fail.

And finally, but certainly not leastly, you must travel at the speed of light. At *least* at the speed of light. Sometimes you might need to travel even faster than light. So always be on the watch. Be ready. Be prepared. Be vigilant. You may be called upon to travel even faster than it is possible for you to travel, in order *to please* God.

Failure to be less than a good angel disappoints God, disappoints fellow angels, and makes you a failure.

Let us pray.

Oh God, our Creator, we confess our failures to you. We have failed you so many times. Ah, but today we renew our angelic vows and ask your forgiveness. Cause us to live as we should. Help us poor angels to be the angels you want us to be.

Amen.

Mrs. Ther listened intently. She was the one person who always *did* listen. And always took every message to heart. A big hot tear came rolling down her face. As the pastor gave an invitation for folks to come forward to rededicate their lives, Mrs. Ther was the first (and only one) to respond. But many came by to shake her hand and encourage her to be an angel. "Alwaze (that was her first name), we will pray for you. God will help you do better," each said encouragingly.

If your minister brought *that* message next Sunday, would you think him quite mad? And if the people sitting out there in the pews accepted his word in the matter, would you not think them also mad? And what of poor Mrs. Ther?

Well, chances are good you did hear just such a message last Sunday! And chances are, most everyone in the audience believed every word that fellow up there said, found nary a fault in his words, and were probably greatly inspired "to do better."

What is wrong here? This: You were being exhorted to be another life form; you were told to do something your life form cannot do and *only* one other life form *can* do. You are not that life form. That fellow up there in front has therefore called you to an impossible thing. You probably also got only an exhortation, one that contained not a clue as to *how* to be an angel.

The supposition was simple: "You *are* an angel. That is all you need. Now go out there and be a good angel."

Your problem is also simple: You can't do what you have been told to do. You are the wrong life form. There is little or nothing that angels, who just happen to live by angel life, can do to be human, or that you can do to be "angel."

Now if you had heard that you must be a human, you could do that. *You organically know* how to live by human life. But angel life is off-limits to you; there is nothing in you that is organically angelic.

Pause for a moment. Just what have *you* been hearing lately? "Be a human"? Unlikely! "Be a good Christian! *Live the Christian life!*" Is that not what you heard last week and almost every Lord's day? And is that not the basic thesis of virtually every religious book you have read? "Go be a good Christian."

Maybe you never thought of it, but "living the Christian life" does not fall into the sphere of the species classified as *Homo sapiens*. When one speaks of "Christian" and "living the Christian life," he is speaking of something not native to humans.

"Christian" is not even *native* to this planet. "Christian" originated outside our biosphere. "Christian" is not found on the biological chart of creatures from this realm. Is "living the Christian life" organic to human life? Or is it possible that "Christian" is something that belongs to a different and higher life form? "Christian" is not angelic; "Christian" is not human. By its very nature, "Christian" is the organic expression of divine life.

Living the Christian life is the exclusive territory of the highest life.

When Jesus Christ got out of bed in the morning, He lived by divine life. *Anything and everything* he did that day fell into the category of *Christian*. The Christian life was organic to His nature. Native, natural, organic—to the life of God. The life form called God (who was once incarnated as a baby in Bethlehem and grew up in Galilee), *He* is what "Christian" is.

God's Son, living by the divine life of His Father that dwelled within Him. *That* is the Christian life. "Living the Christian life" is synonymous with the "outliving" of His life form, and His alone. "Christian" is the *instinctive* expression of *that* form of life.

Conclusion: Only Christ can live the Christian life.

Correct. But here is exciting news. He who is that life form also lives *in* you. Jesus Christ, the highest life, is in you.

Has anyone ever told you that?

You've been exhorted to live the Christian life, but did anyone tell you that Christ *is* the Christian life? Did anyone tell you that He lives in you?

More. Did anyone ever tell you that you can live by Him? But here is the crucial question: After you were converted to Christ, did you get so much as a hint on *how* to live by a life not your own? Or, like Mrs. Ther, were you basically exhorted to be another life form, with no mention being made of *how?*

Without knowing He is in you as a higher life, without knowing *He* is the Christian life, without knowing that He and He alone is the one who lives the Christian life, without knowing how to live by that *life* which is not your own, you might as well be exhorted to be a puppy and live by puppy dog life. Try to live the Christian life solely by your own effort and you will end up feeling you are a buzzard!

You cannot live the Christian life. That is reserved for another life form.

Did anyone ever tell you Christ is in you to be your very life? And if someone did tell you this incredible fact, have you ever had any help in the *how* area?

The instructions we each received as new believers more or less implied, "You are saved; that is the *sole* criterion you need in order to be able to *live the Christian life.*"

Something appears to be missing around here somewhere.

If you tell me that the sole criterion necessary for me to live the Christian life is to get saved, you might as well also tell me I can flap my arms and fly. I cannot. For me to fly, I must have in me the life of a species that flies, and I must also be able to lay hold of that life daily. To live the Christian life I need the life of a species in me who is the Christian life. I must have the highest life, Jesus Christ, in me. And I need to know (I need *desperately* to know) how to live the Christian life. Or better, how to live by His life.

Make it practical to me. Give me the *how,* or stop telling me to live the Christian life. Is knowing you are saved all you need to know to live out the life and experience demanded of those who are the kin of the Living God?

As a young believer (and as a young minister) the closest I ever came to hearing that His life was in me, the closest I ever came to the *how* of living by that life, came to me in one sentence. "Now that you are saved, the Holy Spirit will *enable* you to live the Christian life." That was all. The rest of what I heard was, "To be a good Christian you need to do this and this," and, "Don't do this or this."

Yes, *something* was missing. Desperately missing.

After several years of trying, I found myself asking, "Couldn't you give me just a little bit more help on the *how* part?" But I am not sure that any of my mentors knew any more than I did. Yes, I was told to pray. But if I couldn't pray any better than the fellow who told me to pray, I knew I was in *really* big trouble.

Finally, I made the greatest of all discoveries. I discovered that I cannot live the Christian life!

To ask me to live the Christian life is like asking a pig to live the angel life. The problem with that poor pig is that he is two life forms too far down the biological chart to live the angel life. First that poor pig would need to climb up to human life. Then he would need to climb past human life up to angelic life. Even then he is going to need an awful lot of assistance before he can begin living by a life not his own. Why? Because he is used to being a pig, that's why!

To ask a pig to "live the angel life" is exactly the same as telling me to live the Christian life. I can't. I, too, am two life forms below that possibility.

The first order of business after our salvation must be to learn we have received another life within us. And from that point on, "how to live by a life not our own" must be the highest priority of the new believer's life. (Old believers seem not to know about this either! That pretty well covers just about all of us, dear readers.)

Whatever happened to Mrs. Ther? Well, the last time anyone saw this dear lady, she was on the runway out at the airport. She was trying to travel as fast as an angel. She had just gone through several attempts at becoming airborne and had suffered several runaway heart palpitations. But she had rested up a few moments, rededicated her life, clenched her fists, gritted her teeth, and was heard to say as she galloped down the runway, "I am an angel. I can do it. I can. I can. All I have to do is try harder."

Let us now leave Mrs. Ther, who wishes to move up one place on the biological chart (and pigs, who want to move up *two* places on the biological chart). Let us also leave those who are taking the words of Reverend Trut to heart. Let us now see what a *sardine* can teach us. Or rather, what he can do to help us unlearn some of the things we have been taught about the Christian life.

THIRTEEN

The Seeking Sardine

There once lived a little sardine who did not want to be a sardine. He wanted to be a human. Not a dog, mind you, but a human. He wanted to move up two whole classifications of life. With this ambition burning in him, our disconsolate little sardine began to make inquiries on how to become a human.

His first counsel came from a *red herring*. "So, you wish to be happy, to be the sardine God intended for you to be, and to live for Him?"

"No, I want to be a human," protested the sardine.

"Never mind, the answer is all the same. If you really want to be what God wanted you to be, you need *human* education. Not one of these fish schools, but a *human* university. *Then* you will be the most victorious sardine possible. Remember, if you wish to please God and be all you can be, become the most educated fish in the ocean. Education is essential to the victorious fish . . . er . . . human . . . life."

His second piece of advice came from a *swordfish.*

"The secret to the victorious fish life? Ah, that is simple."

"But I want to be human," protested the little sardine.

"Same thing," said he. "Now listen to me. Read the entire human encyclopedia. Then read it again and again. Then memorize it! That's what you *have* to do. And remember," the swordfish added gravely, "if you don't read it and memorize it, God won't love you."

A big freshwater tear came pouring out of the little sardine's eye. "I have a problem," he said very sadly. "I can't read." He paused and turned away, speaking to himself softly. "Well, first I'll go to a good human university; I'll learn to read, and I'll read and read, and read and read . . . and memorize the whole human encyclopedia. And then God will love me, and *then* I'll be a human!"

The next fish the little sardine encountered was a very solemn-looking *lawbster,* who was solemnly eager to aid the little sardine in his quest to be human.

"The secret to the victorious fish life? There's only one answer! You *must* be the most moral fish in fishdom. And, of course," he said reassuringly, "this is also how you become a human, and how you remain a *good* human.

"First," he said, glaring down at the little sardine ever so sternly, "first, give up those fishy ways of yours. Here, you poor, wretched sardine. Here. See this," he said menacingly as he shoved something at the little sardine. "The four hundred rules, laws, and ordinances you have to do to make God happy. Memorize these! And *never* break a single one of them or you will be in *big* trouble. BIG trouble! Do what I say and you will find out for yourself *this* is how you become a human," he declared, and not without a great sense of satisfaction. "And it's how you *live* by human life, too.

"Remember, keep all the rules, and eventually you will become human. And," he repeated as his voice trailed off, "break them, even *one* of them, and you will never see humandom."

The little sardine was just beginning to try to swallow all this when a beautiful, happy, smiling *goldfish* swam up.

"I hear you are looking for the key to victory," said the goldfish effervescently.

"Well, actually," replied the rather subdued sardine, "I want to be a human, but—"

"Same thing!" interrupted the goldfish. "Let me tell you all about it. It's easy. *Be* positive. Look on the bright side of things. God wants us all to be happy. And," he said, his chest swelled out, *"and* He wants us all to be prosperous! Think nice thoughts. Be kind. Be gentle. And be loving. Always be loving, no matter what. Most of all, see yourself as happy, prosperous, *and* human! Do all this and you'll be transformed into the successful human."

The little sardine couldn't help but be cheered up by so sunny a prospect. He was just about to practice a big large smile when he heard:

Hey you!

"You, sardine! I heard you were looking for *the*

secret. Don't pay any attention to those other fish. *I've* got the secret."

The little sardine wiggle-waggled his way over to the great imposing *mussel* fish. For the next ten minutes the little sardine was challenged, exhorted, and inspired to "evangelize, serve God, give your talents to the Lord, and carry out the Great Fishmission to the uttermost parts of Oceania."

The little sardine was just about to stick out his chest, bow his neck and launch out into an Oceania-wide evangelistic crusade when he heard a:

Psssttt!

"Not true," came a voice filled with both mystery and confidence. "You've heard from the goldfish, the lawbster, and the red herring, haven't you, little sardine?"

"Yes, and the swordfish and the mussel fish, too."

"I've tried their way, too. None of them work. They don't have what you are looking for. I've found the answer. You don't have to be miserable anymore. *This* works."

"Wow!" cried the little sardine. "I'm sure glad to find someone who *knows*. What is the secret? And what kind of fish are you, anyway? I've never seen anything like you. You glow in the dark. Meeting you is electrifying. I think you must *really* have the answer!"

"I am a *glow* fish. And the answer, *the* secret, is your mouth. You have to *speak* human. They have a language, you know. There is a human language," said the glow fish with great wonder, *and* with yet another hint of mystery.

"Speak in human. That's the answer. It gives you victory and power. Think about it. And, you can also be the most powerful sardine in the pond. (Heal all the other sardines!)"

The little sardine was absolutely euphoric as he wiggle-waggled off. "I've got six different possibilities to pursue. One of them is bound to work. I know! I know what I'll do! I'll try all six at once."

Will our little sardine make it? Not a chance. Will he end up frustrated? Absolutely. Discouraged? Bet on it.

The truth is, no sane sardine (or tuna or salmon) would seriously entertain any such advice. A fish is simply the wrong form of life to consider living the human life. Simple *biology* stands in the way of his being human.

And what can our little sardine teach us? That virtually all that is being said to us about *"the* victorious Christian life" is addressed to our human nature. Your human nature is as adept at living the Christian life as a sardine's life is adept at living the human life.

"In order to be a good Christian . . . " is addressing the wrong biological subject, if it is addressing our *Homo sapiens* life. Only *one* life form can live the Christian life. Any other species making an attempt at such a thing is doomed to failure before it begins.

Tell a sardine to be an angel; tell human life to "be" Christian. In either case, you are two classifications short of the capacity to perform. All the morals, rules, calls to duty, guilt, grunts, groans, sweat, steam, willpower, memorizing of verses, or whatever is in vogue these days will help neither you nor a fish to live the Christian life.

The Christian life is, *first,* having the highest life in you. Secondly, living by means of that life. That makes all other offers taste like sea water.

The Lord Jesus' simple message, "I have come that you might have *life,*" makes intellectualism look like ignorance, reveals legalism to be a study in madness, and places speaking in tongues on the back row.

Thank you, little sardine, for teaching us the futility of our life form trying to be another life form, regardless of formulas given. Now, let's see what amazing things a large group of visitors from outer space can show us.

FOURTEEN

Visitors from Outer Space

Have you ever noticed in science fiction stories that visitors from outer space are always technologically (and intellectually) superior to us? They always have a superior spaceship, better weapons, more advanced technology. And their IQ is about four times higher than ours (not to mention that they can always speak *English*). Nothing could reveal more about what we think is *superior.* Superior means, to us, intelligence, technology, and science.

But do you realize that there really is a higher life form *out there?* (I am not speaking of God.) We know their name and their population. And they *are very* superior to us.

Martians? No.

Then what?

The angelic host. They really are superior to humans. (We are created "a little lower than the angels," Heb. 2:7.) And they really are extraterrestrial beings. *And* they sometimes visit this planet.

Now, let's do a little imagining. Let's say the Lord gave about a million angels a temporary leave of absence from the other realm. At the same time He also gave them the ability to stay visible, *and* He gave them permission to visit our galaxy. And He even allowed them to live on a nearby planet.

Ladies and gentlemen, meet real "invaders from outer space." And meet a *big* surprise.

Remember, these particular angels will come to our realm with the same point of view, values, and interests they have always had in their realm.

So, one bright morning, the angels leave the spiritual realm and set down on an uninhabited planet not far from our planetary system. They name their new home ETERNA II. (Our astronomers later gave that planet the title of Palnitus Los Angeles, *not* to be confused with a city by a similar name on TERRA FIRMA I.)

Soon thereafter, our superior neighbors decide to come over and visit *our* planet.

A visit to TERRA FIRMA I! Code name: Operation VLLF III (Visit to Lower Life Form number III).

They let us know ahead of time they are coming. They will set down on the green around Washington Monument, District of Columbia, USA.

Man's fondest dream is about to come true. He gets to meet a race more advanced than his own.

> Arrival time: *12:00 noon*
> Distance traveled: *12 billion light years*
> Length of journey: *.000001 of a second*

Length of stay on TERRA FIRMA I: *A whole day!*

All the dignitaries of earth gather for a most lavish reception.

As out of nowhere, the angels appear.

Because we are all familiar with receptions, yet so unfamiliar with angels, let us eavesdrop on the angels as they look around and get their first impression of us.

Mayor of Washington: It is with great honor that we who are gathered here today welcome our guests from outer space.

(Angelic whispers overheard)

Angels: (They call *this* a reception?)

(This is one drab-looking place.)

(Why don't they turn up the lights?)

(That star up there . . . see. The one that gives off that ugly yellowish glow. I think it's about to go out.)

(They call *this* a reception?)

(With a light no brighter than that, no wonder this place is so dull.)

(Downright dark, if you ask me.)

(They call *this* a reception?)

(This life form surely does move slowly.)

(And talks slowly.)

(They call *this* a reception?)

(They ought to see the reception we throw when one of the redeemed arrive!)

Mayor: Now we would like to show our visitors some of the wonders of our world. We are aware you are advanced far beyond us, so this tour will serve to show you where we are in our stage of evolution. Here, for instance, is our latest in high technology.

Angelic spokesperson: Hmmmm.

Mayor: Look right through here. This astro-telescope is pointed to the farthest distant object we have ever discovered.

Angel: Yes. We stopped off there for a while on our way here.

Mayor: Oh, you have come at a good time. Right now it just so happens we are witnessing the last minute of the last quarter of the most exciting game in all the history of football.

Angel: Hmmmmm.

Mayor: And here you see the largest, most advanced, most academic and scholarly institute of higher learning in all the world.

Angel: Excuse me, Mr. Dignitary, my mind wandered. It's a what?

Mayor: An institute of higher learning. Now, if you will look at our TV monitor, we will show you . . . well, where money is made. See that floor where all those men are yelling and screaming at one another? Well, that is the financial center of the world. *That* is where money is made.

Angel: My, what a curious way to pay homage to an idol—even for heathen. Such utter madness. But the temple the idol is located in looks familiar. Greek Renaissance architecture, I believe. (What did they say was the name of this particular god?)

Mayor: And now, before you go, we have a surprise for you. All the choirs of all the religions *and* all the world have gathered here today in a vast superdome to sing for you. This is the largest choir ever assembled on planet earth. They have chosen to sing for you Handel's "Hallelujah Chorus." Choir, please begin!

Angels: (This is embarrassing.)

(This is *awful.*)

(Try not to show it.)

(This is *really* awful.)

(This is the worst singing I have ever heard.)

(They could at least put their hearts into it.)

(It's over already—that is the shortest song I ever heard.)

(Yes, very short. *Mercifully* short!)

Mayor: Before you leave, could you tell us a little about your planet. Just exactly *how* advanced are you? Where are you technologically?

Angel: Uh, we're not into that.

Mayor: Higher education?

Angel: We must find out what that means.

Mayor: Space travel?

Angel: Yes, a little of that.

Mayor: Sports?

Angel: No.

Mayor: Entertainment?

Angel: Well, yes some. You know how you go to a zoo and laugh at the apes? Well, we sometimes do a little of that, too.

Mayor: At apes?

Angel: No.

Mayor: Then what?

Angel: We'd rather not say.

Mayor: Oh, please. You are among friends.

Angel: Well, it's not that we want to laugh. It's just that sometimes we can't help it.

Mayor: Fine. But what is it that causes you to laugh?

Angel: We had really *rather* not say!

Mayor: Oh, well, uh, what do you higher life forms do?

Angel: We praise.

Mayor: And . . .

Angel: We deliver messages.

Mayor: Is that all?

Angel: No.

Mayor: What then?

Angel: We sing. I mean, *we* really sing!

Mayor: No inventions? No discoveries?

Angel: Oh, yes. Yes, we had an incredible discovery just recently. One of the angels found a whole new octave and two new notes. We must have sung those new notes for a century or two just getting used to them. It was wonderful.

Mayor: That all sounds so . . . *so simple*. Are you *sure* you are a higher life form than we?

Angel: Yes, Mayor. Of *that* we are quite certain.

With that, the angels made their departure, taking a leisurely .000002 of a second to return to ETERNA II.

And what is the point of this fable?

The human soul is into technology, education, success, banking, status, politics, fashion, philosophy, sports, psychology, acceptance, science, approval, intellectualism, talent, theology, speculation, and all the other facets of civilization's multifaceted soulical expressions. But neither the life form just above us nor the life form just below us is interested in any of these things. Dogs, for instance, are not into science and technology. They bark, chase their tails and cats, and bark, and play, and growl, and wag their tails, and bark some more. There is a wide gap between us and what's right under us. Note that their value system and our value system differ greatly.

Furthermore, intellectualism and philosophy do not go any higher on the biological scale. These things *stop* with man. Further up on the biological scale they are unheard of. *All* such things end with us. Education is *not* the highest expression of all things. Braininess, philosophy, education—these are pursuits of, and high values of, a *fallen* people! Do not "Christianize" these things—for example, calling education "Christian." Another example: In the two categories of life above ours, there is no concept of "using your talents to serve the Lord." And the *need* to "give a *rational* explanation for your faith" is a value from our lower position on the biological scale; and, of course, so is the seminary in which it is taught.

We have picked up an awful lot of extrascriptural ideas. We have picked them up from places other than His Spirit in our spirit, *and* from places other than Holy Writ.

For instance, we ascribe to God the kind of superiority that science fiction ascribes to beings of higher intelligence. Therefore, if we are to understand God, we need a college education plus a master's degree.

Dear reader, that is *not* how you get to know God.

Observe, please, that as life moves up the biological scale, the things of the soul become secondary and the things of the spirit become central. You will never get an angel, who is one up on us, excited about "a good education"; he is no more into that than a puppy is. Nor will you find an angel trying to produce a better automobile or television; nor will you find him on an assembly line producing exotic electronics. Neither will you find him striving for a four-bedroom house, three cars, and a boat!

We also need to recall that until the last 150 years, illiteracy ran from 85 to 99 percent of the human race. Just how long has the human race been that illiterate? Since the dawn of recorded history. Point: The Christian faith can be known in all its depth, glory, and fullness without scholarship, intellectualism, higher education, or being highly gifted. Having a high IQ has nothing to do with how well you can know the Lord. Jesus Christ is known and encountered deep within the inmost depths of your *spiritual* being, not in your frontal lobe. Even being able to read is not a criterion for the deeper Christian life. He is known within. And "within" refers to "within your spirit," not "within your brain."

Do not confuse the values of the human soul with the organic nature of your redeemed and resurrected spirit.

The human soul is just that: Human. Earthly.

This most marvelous and precious of all earthly creation . . . the soul . . . daily carries out its function: to communicate with oneself; to communicate with others; to communicate with one's surroundings; and to carry on the responsibilities of an occupation. But to feed the soul with the upper stratosphere of man's intellectual reaches does not make him spiritual. No, such things only make the power of his soul *exotic*.

The first order of the believer is to get to know a living, redeeming, transforming Lord and Savior named the Lord Jesus Christ who lives in him.

Let dogs bark, let angels hasten, let man so sharpen his powers of the soul that they *appear* to be taking on attributes of the spirit. In the meantime, let us ordinary Christians who have an IQ of about 100 and who find Aristotle dreadfully dull and a Ph.D. in philosophy and another in theology *less* than necessary in order to know the Lord, let us peasants of the faith do what we are supposed to do . . . let us, together, know our Lord!

If the angels and the puppies have anything to tell us, it is this. Whether you are white, black, or purple; be you liberal or conservative, artistic or color-blind, male or female; regardless of your education, your social standing, your economic strata, your goals, your ambitions, your political beliefs, or your cultural background, *if* you should begin to touch that *other* life that is in you, and *if* you should begin to live by that higher life, expect a revolution in your value system. It is a higher life in angels that causes them not to make electronic gadgets. Expect a higher life in you to revolutionize *everything* within the matrix of your life.

In the next chapter we will be looking at the bio-*zoe*-ological composition of:

> Unfallen Adam
> Fallen Adam
> The whole race of the fallen species
> The Lord Jesus Christ while on earth
> The resurrected Christ
> The redeemed as they are now
> The Lord Jesus in glory*

---

* See addendum I for more on the biological uniqueness of Jesus Christ.

PART 4

FIFTEEN

The Biological Chart

I have spoken of the Christian as actually a distinct species, apart from the unbeliever. Is this valid? Yes, insofar as we, like the electric eel, have "parts" in us not found in the non-Christian.

Paul speaks of us as being a new creation. He also declares us to be a "new man." (The word in Greek means "a new human," or "a new humanity"—that is, a human distinctly unlike those referred to as the *old* man, or old humanity.)

Second-century Christian writers actually referred to believers as "the new race" or "the third race," that is, not Jew nor Gentile.

Here is a brief look at the first creation and the new creation from a biological view.*

---

* Remember that we are using the terms *biology* and *biological* in a special way as defined in chapter 1. See pages 6-7.

Unfallen Adam: An innocent body and a perfectly innocent soul. Adam was as perfect as God could make a man *without* having placed God's life in him. He had a spirit that had its origins in the spiritual realm. His habitat was the Garden of Eden.

This species was not supposed to remain in the first state. He had not been completed. He had been created to have God's life in him. *This* species, in this unfinished stage, was *never* intended to become a race of people.

Fallen Adam: A body indwelt by sin, a soul scarred by sin, damaged in nature and lost from God. A dead spirit, causing Adam to be cut off from the realm of things spiritual—that is, cut off from the riches of the heavenly places that are in Christ Jesus (Eph. 1:2-3).

The Fallen Race of the Sons of Adam: The body has been so corrupted by sin, it is now "flesh." Man is primarily under the control of sin indwelling the body . . . that is, the flesh. The soul is enlarged, seeking (but failing) to take over the function of the spirit. The spirit is dead to spiritual things, and man is estranged from God.

Jesus Christ, God's Only Begotten Son, While on Earth: A sinless body, a perfect soul, and a perfectly balanced spirit. A living spirit. The very life of the Father and the Holy Spirit indwelling him and one with Jesus' spirit.

The Resurrected Christ: The same as above, except His physical body has in some way taken on the attribute of also being spiritual. He has passed through death in His spirit, His soul, and His body. He is perfect in His physical being and His spiritual being, and is transcendent above the space-time creation.

The Believer: The spirit has been made alive. The believer is now indwelt and made one with Jesus Christ within the spirit of the believer. The soul is forgiven, cleansed, and other marvelous things. Most of all, the soul is being transformed. When fully transformed, it appears that it will have the properties of that which is spiritual. The body is still a mess, waiting for the return of Jesus Christ when it shall be *changed.*

The Glorified Christ: The One now reigning in the heavenlies (yet inside each and every believer), this One is indescribable, as John proved when he attempted to describe Him!

The *resurrected* believer, *after* the Lord returns? We do not know the answer to that. But we have incredible hope . . . because

> We know not what we shall be,
> but
> we shall be like Him!

In part five we will look at the place where we are supposed to go, as believers, to experience the deeper Christian life.

PART 5

SIXTEEN

The Founding of a Habitat for Our Species

Every species has a habitat uniquely different from that of any other life form. But one day a life form invaded this planet who had no natural habitat here on this planet. However, He meant to change that. He had very definite plans to create a habitat particularly and peculiarly perfect for His species. He had come from a very special kind of matrix and he meant to have a similar habitat on this blue-green ball. He would have a habitat *here* even if it meant bringing His natural habitat—which was in another realm— through the Door between the two realms and placing that habitat right here on earth. One way or another, the other species and the other inhabitants of this old planet were due to see the arrival of both a new species *and* a totally new kind of habitat for a unique species.

This invader from "above" often referred to the place where He had formerly lived. Change one word, from *kingdom* to *habitat,* and you will see just how serious He was about establishing a *place* here on earth where He could live.

> I am not of this world.
> My habitat is not of this world.
> My habitat is near.
> Seek My habitat and all these things will be added.
> I will drink this cup with you again in My Father's habitat.
> My Father desires to give you *His* habitat.
> We will join Him in His habitat as sons, there to enter into the eternal habitat.
> You have inherited *His* habitat.
> God's own habitat has come to you.
> The mystery of My habitat will be yours.
> If you look back, you are not fit for My habitat.
> You will sit down and eat bread in My Father's habitat.
> No one will see My habitat when it is established here.
> I am from above.
> You must be born from above or you cannot see My habitat.
> Only if the Spirit is in you can you go into the habitat of God.
> Those who continue to be seekers in their spirit, *they* are the ones who get God's habitat!

This place for the new species to live was very important to your Lord.

Never think that your habitat (created specifically for your species) is unimportant. Like any other living thing, your survival and my survival as spiritual beings is dependent on our having a proper habitat. Take away the natural habitat of any species, force that species to live in an unnatural habitat, and you doom that species to extinction, or to an existence not much better than death. Are we here to be in a habitat not much more attractive than a cage? Or, even while here on earth, shall we explore the eternals with Him, in His habitat? It was for freedom He set us free!

If we, the believers, are truly biologically unique; and if we, the believers, really are a new creation; if our species really has only recently been introduced to this planet; if we really are a species with a right to both realms, if we are made up of "parts" from both realms; then seeking out, finding, and living in our natural habitat is absolutely crucial to our existence.

You can even guess what it will be like. The Lord Jesus is One who belongs to both realms. (So also are we.) So we can expect this habitat to be made up partly of elements from this realm and partly of elements from the other realm.

Now what of this brand-new species? Shall we become part and parcel of the habitat of the old, fallen, and unbelieving man? Shall we borrow a habitat from another species? Well, their habitat does not *fit* us. Besides, it is against nature to borrow another matrix. No, the new species that began to multiply on the earth just after the Resurrection was destined to a totally new habitat unlike anything else this world had ever seen.

Fallen man and this new creature do *not* share a common habitat. Repeat: our habitat and the old man's habitat are not the same.

The first one of our species came to this earth and for thirty-three years lived here, alone. He had no other members of His "race." Yet, as we have seen, the facets of fallen man's civilization in no way attracted Him. To Him, "civilization" was an idea that belonged to a lower life form!

Many men thought He would set up a new habitat in Israel, that He would erect a throne, that he would overthrow Rome and inaugurate a new nation where His unique species would live. But by a lower form of life! Rome, Italy, Syria, Greece, Israel, Egypt, etc. . . . none of the boundaries of these nations had any influence on what His habitat would be like or where He would establish it. Then what *did* influence Him in the establishing of a habitat for His species?

There was a very *definite* influence! Special ingredients molded the features of His domicile. What were they?

More than anything else, His past experience in eternity molded His design for a habitat here on earth. Powerful influences were at work in this greatest of all architects. His internal instincts. His *former* experiences where He had lived before coming here. Life in the spiritual realms. The fact that He was very God of very God and also totally man—this paradoxical unity influenced what His habitat would be.

These are the ingredients that influenced the

design of the habitat *He* established. He established this habitat with two people in mind: Himself and you. His instincts were heavenly and divine. The major features of our habitat had belonged to the other realm. He had lived in the realm of the invisibles, in places where the Living God made His habitat. He brought those elements together and designed and built a habitat for us who are native to the physical realm.

Certainly the place where He had formerly lived was unlike anything fallen man had ever seen. The two habitats of these two species are incomparable! Incredibly so. In His heavenly abode there were no boundaries to His habitat. It was free of time, free of space. There were no racial distinctions, but there was citizenship! Until now, citizenship in that habitat had been limited to only three—God the Father, God the Son, and God the Holy Spirit. A small citizenship indeed.

The citizenship of that habitat greatly increased on the day of Pentecost. After thirty-three years on this planet, wandering around without a habitat and without any other members of His species, He suddenly had lots of fellow citizens. And they had a place—a place where all could live together. He established His own species, then He gave them a habitat!

And sure enough this new man, this head of a new kind of race, set up a habitat that matched the new species. Notice: birds belong to the sky, fish to the water, cattle to the field. Habitat and creature match. God, who is a spirit and invisible, belongs to the realm of the spirituals and the invisibles.

What of this One and His species? As we have seen, He belongs to both realms. So do we. He had lived in the bosom of His Father for all eternity past, and then for thirty-three years He lived in the visible realm. Expect the habitat to match the species. That habitat, by its very nature, must have in it both a touch of the heavenlies and a touch of earth, partially of the invisibles and the spirituals, and partially of the physical and the spiritual.

Your Lord combined the elements of His past experience in the spiritual realm with the elements of His thirty-three-year experience in the visible, physical realm. He created a habitat combining two realms. It is in that incredible place that His new creation dwells.

A species always, instinctively, seeks out and *knows* its natural habitat. God puts an organic instinct in every creature to find its normal habitat. You will long for this place as long as you live!

One sheep alone can never survive. And if he could survive *alone,* still his living would never make any sense. He *has* to live in a flock. God made him that way. A flock is organic to a sheep. Fish live in schools. Pull a fish out of that school and put him on his own, and his life will not make sense and his chances of survival are nil. The lion must have his pride, or even he will be prey to predators of the jungle. Even the mighty elephant instinctively knows that he belongs within the elephant herd, there to find protection, fulfillment, and meaning.

Even your Lord was biologically driven to the habitat that He created for the new species. Once He began His ministry on this earth, even the Son of

God/Son of Man naturally drew around Him men and women who had deep, profound longings to touch the realm of the spirituals. They belonged together. All were on earth. *All* wanted a touch with the reality of that other realm. Note that it was He who decided just how close He and His followers would live during those three years. *Community* was God's idea. And it was your Lord who "invented" *fellowship*. (Actually, He introduced it to our planet. *Fellowship* is and always has been the number one activity of the God-head.) They lived in close-knit proximity to one another, a community of the redeemed, for three years.

As time passed, those who lived with Him, that is, those who lived with divinity, began to sense that *He* was in constant touch with *both* realms at the same time.

But what of them? What would happen after He ascended and they remained on earth? What would be their habitat? Once He left them alone, they came to realize that they, too, were creatures of both realms. And truly they had a burning instinct for their natural habitat.

Yes, His followers had been born on this earth. But something else had happened to these men and women after the resurrection. They had also been "born from above." Every one of them had two birthdays, one for each of the two realms. This is what made them unique to other creatures here on this planet.

But you and the rest of your species have a burning desire to leave this old creation. To leave and go to the new creation. But the new creation (the new heaven and the new earth) isn't here yet! Where does this new biological life form live until the Lord's return? Where will they live until this old creation dissolves and a new heaven and a new earth come into existence?

One thing is certain: This people will live in a flock, a herd, a fold, a school, a tribe, a gaggle, or a *something!* Members of this new species will not live independently.

And back there on the day of Pentecost, they were not about to borrow someone else's habitat. This new species was interdependent. The Father, the Son, and the Holy Spirit, the progenitors of their race, had long ago set the standard for their habitat. In heaven and on earth, the Lord Jesus had lived in "community"! Actually He brought to earth, out of heaven, something that this planet would one day call "ecclesia."

The idea and practice of ecclesia is as old as the Trinity!

After the resurrection, those first believers did not forget. They had sojourned together with Him for three years. By sheer instinct (and by their own past experiences) these men and women were driven to search out the habitat to which they belonged, to continue to live with Him, and with one another. And on the day of Pentecost they got this totally new kind of habitat.

It was there in that revolutionary habitat that they and others of their species learned to know an indwelling Lord and to live by Him. Living by the highest life was always a "together" experience.

Where does that leave us today? Let us see.

SEVENTEEN

The Evangelical Blind Spot

We evangelicals generally do not have the foggiest idea what seeking to know the Lord *together* means. Ever since we evangelicals emerged during the Reformation, we have been *without* a habitat.

How so?

One hour on Sunday morning and maybe an hour and a half on Wednesday night, the majority of evangelical Christians just check into a building with a high roof and a spire on top. There they say hello to the other members of their species, and that is it! At the end of sitting on a pew for an hour or so, they say good-bye. After that, each one is on his own. And without knowing it, each of us is like that little sheep that got separated from the flock. No other species, unless it is animals held in a zoo, is so utterly without a habitat as we are!

No wonder we are spiritual basket cases! We believers are cut off from our natural habitat. Shall it ever be so?

Thank God, Simon Peter knew what his habitat was. The Twelve also remembered. The 120 remembered, too. All the believers of the first century knew what their natural habitat was. Take a new look at the New Testament and you will see just how attached they were to their native "home."

May I illustrate.

We always read Matthew, Mark, Luke, and John *first* when going through the Scripture. But these are not the first and oldest parts of the New Testament. Most of the Epistles were written *before* the four Gospels, and they were written to the ecclesia, not to the individual. The same is true of the four Gospels. The events recorded in the Gospels came first; but they were written a bit later, for the benefit of the ecclesia, not for the individual.

Your Lord's life on this planet was lived primarily in an enclave of believers. He lived here in a traveling community of believers. They lived with Him. Later, they together lived by Him and for Him. It was always a *plural* experience.

Did the *oldest* pieces of Christian literature reflect this same "let's get to know the Lord *together*" attitude? Was there anything of the solo mind-set among first century believers? Let's take a look at the Epistles, especially Paul's letters.

Were the first pieces of Christian literature addressed to an individual? (That is the way we generally read them.) Or were these writings for the community of believers? Were they first penned for you, the individual? No, dear evangelical Protestant. *No!* That literature was not written for you, nor for me. And despite the fact we almost always deal with those letters as though they were written to an individual, and despite the fact our mind-set can hardly conceive of a piece of Christian literature being written to a community, that literature was addressed *to the habitat.*

Look first at Galatians, for it well may be the first piece of Christian literature ever penned. You and I have been trying to wring that book dry in order to get every drop of blessing it contains: blessing *for you, for me.* But it was written to the *whole* habitat, and it really makes no sense except as it is seen written to an "us," not a "me."

Perhaps right now you belong to a group. A nonprofit, tax-exempt religious organization? If so, then you are probably going through the Bible trying to find your organization on every page! But that book is not written for either you or your organization!

Galatians was written to communities of believers. To the ecclesia. *That* book was addressed to the whole, corporate habitat. Outside the natural, organic habitat of our species, that book cannot convey its intended practical significance for our spiritual lives. Your Lord did not write that book to individuals. The whole New Testament was addressed almost exclusively to those within a *habitat* of the redeemed!

But what about all the riches found in First and Second Thessalonians (the second-oldest pieces of Christian literature)? Those two books were also written to a community of believers living within their organic habitat.

Then what about First and Second Corinthians?

Sorry. Both books were written, not to a single individual, but to an ecclesia, to a group of the new species who were living together in their *flock,* their *nation,* their *school,* their *covey.* Both were written for those who live together in the utterly unique kingdom, a kingdom that had invaded this planet from out of another realm.

But what about Colossians? And Philippians? And Ephesians? Aren't those written for you, the individual? Absolutely not. Every one of them was written to the community of the believers, to the habitat! Not to that sheep that had wandered off from the flock and was trying to get by without the other sheep.

But what about the book of Romans? It was written to a *group of believers* who were meeting in the home of Priscilla and Aquila in the Italian city of Rome. Not to religious organizations. Not to you, the independent, evangelical Protestant believer.

Furthermore, the promises made in those letters will fall short if you try to make them apply to you, the individual. They were written, addressed to, and filled with promises and revelation specifically for a corporate community. For the habitat.

Again, no wonder the Christian life doesn't work very well. We are each not unlike an elephant in a zoo trying to be a herd of elephants! No elephant in a zoo has ever known true elephant life and never will until someone lets it rejoin its herd back there in Africa!

Ah, but what about First and Second Timothy and Titus? Now there are books really written to *individuals.* Yes, dear reader, and who are those individuals? They were young men who were out *establishing* a habitat for the redeemed. They were *ecclesia planters!* And the contents of those letters deal specifically with things involved in establishing a habitat for those who belong to our particular biological species.

That leaves you with the book of Philemon. At last! There *is* a book in the New Testament that is *just for you,* the *individual.* And the next time you have a runaway slave, by all means, read this letter!

First-century believers saw the entire Christian faith from the view of a habitat. What happened? How did we lose it? Can we get it back?

EIGHTEEN

The Place to Go to Learn How to Live by His Life

There is a specific place to go to learn how to live by a life not your own. There is a place to learn about the deeper Christian life. It is really the *only* place God ever intended for you to learn how to live the Christian life. The living of the Christian life, and the learning of that life, are *inseparable* from that place. From the very beginning of our species (called "Christian"), our ancestors lived in an environment that was native to man's very instincts.

Unfortunately, we lost this place. It has been lost to most of us for the better part of 1,700 years. That loss is perhaps the clearest explanation as to why living out the Christian life has been so elusive to us. The loss occurred about three hundred years after Pentecost. That was a very long time ago. At that time we Christians, somewhat like Adam, got pushed out of our *natural* environment.

Tragically, most of us today are unaware of this sad event. Nor do we have any idea what an impact it has had on our lives. Tragically, we have never returned to our organic habitat.

We are just about the only species on earth whose almost entire population is cut off from our natural place of living. The problems faced in reclaiming our habitat are formidable. We have settled down in the habitat of fallen man; furthermore, we keep on being told that our habitat is something that it is *not*. In fact, we are constantly being bombarded with a sales campaign that tells us this artificial, uncomfortable, boring habitat we *are* in is our natural habitat.

The return to the place we were intended to live is high on the list of priorities for those seeking to live the highest life.

Things were quite different for a believer in the first three centuries of our faith. But attempting to describe to someone today what the habitat of early believers was like is almost impossible. The reason for the difficulty is simply that we have no word in our language today that conveys the meaning of *their* experience. (We once had a word, but its original meaning has been totally altered—so altered that using that word increases the communication problem. It is a word we do *not* want to use if we are trying to communicate the experience of early believers and to describe their natural habitat. We end up, therefore, searching for other words to use. But all the words we come up with are inadequate.)

Gaining an insight into the matrix of the early

believers ultimately boils down to discovering your own internal, spiritual *instinct* for that habitat. Those instincts *are* there, operating in you, *now*. And if you should ever see your habitat, those instincts would soar.

What *was* our habitat before we lost it?

Well, in the first century, being a *believer* and being in *that habitat* were synonymous. In fact, the habitat is what *defined* what the followers of Christ were to the rest of the world. It was not just their belief in Christ that made them different. Nor was it that the individuals had been radically changed by Jesus Christ. Rather, in the eyes of both the world and in the eyes of the believer, it was mostly the way they all stuck together.

The believers and their habitat—they were one and the same. This single/dual witness is what really intrigued, mystified, mesmerized, offended, and attracted the unbeliever. The habitat of the redeemed was like nothing anyone had ever seen. The heathen were intrigued and outraged at those believers and their odd "way of life."

What, then, was that habitat? This is a difficult question. The answer remains difficult to communicate. Better we begin by asking, What was it not?

The habitat of the early believers was not some retreat into the mountains or the wilderness, there to escape the world, raise their kids away from decadence, grow organic vegetables, and wear long beards and floor-length dresses. Escaping from the riot, crime, and sin of man and his civilization, which was falling apart, was *not* what the early believers did. Such an idea was totally outside the mind of the ancient believer. Rather, those hardy folk set up their habitat right in the middle of the *old man's* civilization and then proceeded to ignore it!

Civilization is an international interlocking of all of the systems of fallen man. Paradoxically, the individuals who are within that system are both utterly dependent on that system and totally caught up in it, and at the same time they live a life fiercely independent of one another.

The believers' habitat had no national or international interlocking. Their habitat was local in nature. Just local gatherings. On occasion, they had contact with other believers from other places.

All believers were found in this habitat. All were very close to one another. They held on to one another. Their togetherness was as thick as molasses. There was no special building involved. They were *inter*dependent on one another (and on the Lord).

Their habitat was in full operation twenty-four hours per day. It was filled with love and caring. There was also a fantastic amount of spiritual experience going on among them. Daily. Yes, *daily* there was a touch with an indwelling Lord in the lives of *each* believer, and among *all* the believers.

Trying to find a word today to describe that long lost experience is difficult. We struggle with terms such as *corporate living* and *the life of the ecclesia*. We also try new words such as *gathering* and *meeting,* though both are terribly inadequate. We use *Christian community* or just *community*. In trying to describe this habitat, you might use the original word from its original language—*ecclesia*. However, using the English translation of that word causes a total collapse in what one is seeking to communicate.

Anyway, our *natural* habitat is *not* what we are constantly being told it is. It is *not* getting together one hour on Sunday morning. Sadly, when believers were pushed out of their habitat and into government-sponsored, government-erected buildings, that concept of seeing one another and being together a few moments every week is the very concept that replaced the meaning of the word *ecclesia,* as it had been understood by the believers.*

One solemn hour together each week, then six days and twenty-three hours lived in the civilization of fallen man, was *not* the earlier believers' understanding of ecclesia. They had their own community, they *were* their community. They had their own "civilization." It operated around the clock and throughout the calendar.

We are faced with a problem of monumental proportions: *how* to discover just what our habitat is.

Important?

The Christian life may never really make sense without it. The Christian today who is seeking to grow in Christ has just possibly never heard about this habitat and surely does not know he needs it. Yet he longs for it, instinctively. But a believer will never *really* want that habitat (no matter how hard one tries to describe it) until he experiences it! And that experience is rare. Saying it is hard to find is being optimistic.

Anyway, a life lived in love and care, a life lived in close proximity to others, a life of experiencing

---

* See addendum IV for more on what happened to our habitat after Constantine.

Christ together, internally and corporately, was the *Christian life* during those early days of our faith.

Constantine changed all that! When he took the throne of the Roman Empire, less than 4 percent of that empire was Christian. Before he came along, believers gathered in homes and lived in enclaves. But by the time of the death of the Emperor Constantine, just about *everyone* was a "Christian." And that, dear reader, is just *too* many Christians.

The other tragedy was that the *state* (the Roman Empire) began building places for believers to meet. These buildings were built at the state's expense and *given* to the Christians as a gift.

The pagan mentality of that time saw "religion" as being people reporting to a pagan temple once or twice a week, standing around an altar watching a group of solemn-faced, darkly dressed priests offer a sacrifice to a heathen god. When the ritual was over, everyone went home! *This* mind-set eventually prevailed in Christendom. The corporate nature of the ecclesia was lost. Community ended. The enclaves disappeared. The natural habitat of our species vanished. And the proper place to learn how to live by the Lord's life vanished with it.

In that loss, you and I suffered *almost* irreparable spiritual loss.

Let the record show that this book you are now reading does not suggest to you, the believer, that it is a workable concept to hope for living by the highest life outside the organic habitat for that life. For most of us, it simply is not workable. A steam engine will not run on sand, nor an internal combustion engine on water. And for those believers who are like you and me, *ordinary* people, not *unusual* believers, this matter of living the Christian life simply does not pan out in an isolated situation. Nor does it work in a typical go-to-church-on-Sunday situation.

Alas, dear reader, I hate to tell you this, but our "engine" will not ever run well on "where two or three are gathered," or on a home Bible class, or home fellowship meetings. The Christian life has to do with a life form, yes; but it also has to do with the *habitat* of that life form.

How long can a newly born lamb "live the sheep life" by itself? Until it meets its first bear, or needs its first drink of water, or encounters its first lion. A lamb survives and thrives only within its natural habitat.

As much as we evangelical believers may hate to admit it, we need the corporateness of the body of Christ—day and night. A dog or a wolf may survive alone . . . barely. But it is against nature to try to do so. (The ever-independent cat can survive on its own and *flourish!* But we are not cats.) *We are lambs!* Fragile, weak lambs! And we are lambs without any great willpower. Survive we *might,* but the living out of our spiritual destiny is not intended for one alone. Living by the highest life is a venture lived out among a community of a committed *body* of believers. Come glory, come gore, come blessing, come drought, come hell or high water, come feast or famine, believers are a people who are in this thing together, around the clock, through the calendar, for all the rest of their lives.

So it was in the beginning. So may it be again.

NINETEEN

The Land of Ecclesia

The kingdoms of this planet are located on specific plots of ground. Birds, on the other hand, never will be confined to the boundaries of man's nations. Nor will boundaries dictate to us. Our "flock" gathers anywhere. If our species is found in a certain city or nation, it is our instinct to gather together. Geographic boundaries set up by bees, or ants, or man, or anything else, do not stop us.

Our nation is not patterned after the nations of men, for within our organic habitat we are each under the *direct* headship of the Lord. Not chains of command, but biological order. As in a family . . . organic.

Our species gathers by instinct. We share. Sing. Worship our King and follow Him as He speaks within each of our spirits. Our species takes care of one another. We love one another. But not with human love. Rather, with that love that belongs to the highest life form.

It is easy to describe the atmosphere within this habitat. It has a touch of earth, but it also has a touch of heaven. It is an interface: It is a place where the spiritual realm and the physical realm overlap. In that place of overlapping, *that* is where our species lives.

It is there you learn to live by the highest life, which has been implanted within you. Like Simon Peter, you have *already* become partaker of the divine nature, but in that habitat you will learn how to find your spirit, understand its ways, and after a time come to know the distinction of mind, will, and emotions, as over against your spirit. You are not gathering there primarily to learn power, visions, dreams, prophecies, miracles, signs, wonders. Those are common things that believers in every generation have had in abundance. Rather, you will learn something that is *very* rare: The word is *fellowship*. The learning of it takes a bit of time. Fellowship with the other believers, yes. But much, much more than that.

Fellowship with Jesus Christ.

That last sentence is *not* a reference to prayer. (That is, not the getting-down-on-your-knees-every-morning-and-praying-for-an-hour kind of prayer.) Rather, it is *fellowship* somewhat like Adam had in the garden, something that Jesus Christ did all day long as He lived in the presence of His Father and there fellowshiped with His own *indwelling* Lord.

Perhaps the first business that goes on inside the habitat of our species is learning how to fellowship with the Lord Jesus Christ. That is a rare thing, and it is an activity confined solely to our kind.

Gradually, you will learn to live by *His* implanted life. *This* is the major occupation within the habitat of our species. *Not* service, *not* obligation, *not* morals, *not* laws, *not* orders, *not* commands, *not* forms. *Fellowship* with Him.

You learn this internal fellowship with Him, *not alone,* but with others, with members of *your* species. With the weak, those not strong in self-discipline. With the morally damaged, those not inclined to be spiritual. With the *non*special people, not just the highly gifted believers. With others just like you!

Please remember what this book has said: Seeking to learn to live by the highest life without ever having been shown *how,* trying to set up lines of communication with the Lord Jesus Christ, trying all this without your brothers and sisters around you, trying without being constantly surrounded by others, trying without being consistently engaged in the enterprise of knowing Him with others . . . will almost certainly bring disappointment.

So what shall be your course, dear member of a new creation?

If you are young, if you have only recently met Christ, then you are very blessed. You have not yet learned how to do things the wrong way. Like the ugly duckling, you only need to figure out that a duck you are not. You are a swan. Go. Live by swan life. Stay in the company of other swans. You are biologically different from ducks. Let the ducks take care of their own problems; you have swans to live with. There, among them, live by swan life.

Where do you go to run around with other such creatures? Even to live out the rest of your life with them? What is the name of this habitat, this glorious nation, this citizenship composed of those who are members of God's own family?

Well, the place you are looking for is called *the ecclesia*. The gathering of God's people. The church. But it is the church twenty-four hours a day, seven days a week. That is the kingdom as it is known and experienced on this planet, *now!*

A foretaste. A foretaste of that which is to come. And what is to come? More of the same, pressed down and running over. Today it is the ecclesia. Tomorrow she shall be a city and a bride. No other life form on this planet has anything remotely similar to a habitat like ours! Hallelujah!

As a believer in Christ, you really have only two things to do: (1) learn to live by the very life of God; and (2) live that life together with those who also have that same, highest life in them.

This all takes time, a great deal of time. Three or four years will just get you started. To fully grow into this business of Christ being your life, how long does that take? About the length of one lifetime. Sorry, transformation really does take time. That is the way your Lord has chosen it to be. This fact is a little hard for believers to swallow, especially if they are Americans. We want instant everything. There is no "add water and stir" to *this* gospel. Furthermore, there is no shortcut to transformation, no *single* experience known to man—not the Pentecost experience, not the Easter experience, not the Christmas experience, not the Happy New Year experience, not the Fourth of

July experience, or any other experience that some-one out there will surely try to sell you—that will shorten the time necessary to grow fully into the reality of the depths of Jesus Christ. There is simply not *anything* that will hurry this rather slow process.

What can you expect to happen to you as a result of living by the highest life?

That answer is so easy to give. Expect to have happen to you just about everything that happened to your Lord, Jesus Christ. The glory, the wonder, the fellowship He knew with the Father who lived inside Him. (And the added fellowship you will know as you fellowship with both the Father and the Son who live within you.)

You see, your Lord is not only the first of this new species, He is also the pathfinder. *He* is the history of this life. Whatever happened to Him while He was on earth—whatever He experienced here on this planet while living by the life of His Father—*that* is more or less *your* destiny also. Whatever His experience, whatever His history, whatever happened to Him within His experience of *that* higher life will in some way or another probably be experienced by you, or by someone close to you (someone who shares the same habitat with you). The Lord's *internal* experience, while living on this earth, will also be your internal experience while living on this earth. His spiritual history will become your spiritual history.

I will close then, dear reader, with one thing that you should seriously consider ere you venture out upon this, the greatest odyssey of all. Remember that whatever this adventure brings into your life, it was His will and it *is* His will for you. Be careful before you decide to take this journey, for included in the very nature of *His* life are many, many things. And one of those things is the cross.

Living by the highest life will almost certainly get you crucified.

The length of time involved, the need of being in ecclesia, and the virtual assurance of experiencing *at least* one first-class crucifixion are some of the things you must seriously ponder.

Are you sure this is *really* what you want?

If your final resolution is a yes, then don't just sit there. Find others with the same heart's desire and join the rest of your species in the Land of Ecclesia!

ADDENDA

The Biological Uniqueness of Jesus Christ and the Believer

When God came to earth in the likeness of human flesh, He showed us the vast biological gap between divine life and human life.* He also showed us the vast values gap, the life-style gap, as well as the political, governmental, and educational gaps. When this one named Jesus lived by divine life, everything He did and said showed to us all the cavernous dissimilarity between these two life forms.

The intellect, science, theology, and countless other areas of the old species seemed to have no place of overlap with this biologically dissimilar being.

Let us go to the heart of the matter. The way each species apprehended (laid hold of) that which was

---

* See chapter I to understand how the terms *biology* and *biological* are used in this book.

going on in them and around them was in two totally separate spheres.

Let us look at some of the elements at work in His life that are totally missing in the third-highest life.

Others are led by their soul; He is led by His spirit. The spirits of other men were filled with death inherited from Adam. Jesus' spirit was alive, and it was filled with the divine Holy Spirit (Luke 4:1).

There was an opening between this realm and the other realm. The opening was for Him! He could hear and see things come from that realm. Things that had their origin and habitat in the other realm came through that opening in order to come to Him (Matt. 3:16).

Even creations from the other realm slipped through that passage—left open for Him—to come and care for Him (Matt. 4:11).

Incredibly, He told a man not only what the man was thinking; He told *that* man that *he* would one day see the unseen (John 1:51).

He knew exactly where fish were (Luke 5:4-7).

Other men thought with their intelligence. Jesus went far higher than that; He perceived (Luke 5:22).

He knew that He had previously lived in another realm, that He was from that realm, that the other realm was a higher realm than this one, and that, because He was from that realm, He was "above" the things of this realm. He also stated that He had *seen* and He had *heard* the things that were in the other realm. Furthermore, what He had seen and heard there were the things He talked about here (John 3:31; 8:26, 40; 15:15).

John the Baptist declared that the Spirit in Jesus

was limitless and immeasurable, that this Spirit caused Him to hear what God said and that the things *He* heard were the only things He spoke (John 3:31-34).

The Lord Jesus could look at a woman, tell how many husbands she had (she had had five!), and that she had been elected by His Father to receive the highest life (John 4:16-18).

He also knew that He was about to begin a new order. The place His followers were going to worship God was inside their living spirits (John 4:23-24). He also knew He had been sent here to seek out those whom His Father was seeking. He came to find those who would worship His Father inside their inmost being.

He knew (that is, He had an experiential knowing) that men were plotting to kill Him (Matt. 12:15).

The covered was revealed, the hidden was known. He had things operating in Him unknown to mortal men (Luke 12:2).

God the Father will be in the believer and will know the believer's needs before the believer knows them (Matt. 6:4, 6, 8).

He placed great value on the other realm, then declared that the other realm was *in* Him. Then He stated that this very realm would also be *in* the believer! That treasure could be placed there. He told them to seek and find that realm! He told them where it was—inside of them (Matt. 6:19ff.; 6:33).

He expected His followers to be able to hear and see and *perceive* what others could not (Matt. 13:14, 16; Luke 8:46). He stated that the believer could not only *see* the other realm; one had to be born in it. You could know you had that birth. That realm exists in a way similar to how you know the wind exists (John 3:8).

Jesus declared He had lived in the other realm, had come down from out of that realm, was going back to that realm, and even as He sat talking, He was in that other realm at that very moment (John 3:13). Furthermore, if He spoke of that realm, the unregenerate man could not ever understand things that were of that realm (John 3:12)!

He declared He was from "above," the same place where His followers would be born. "Above!" (John 3:3, 31; 8:23; 19:11).

"Above" seems to be a very important place!

The Lord had an almost overwhelming sense of where He came from, and a sense that most men on this earth did not understand and would *never* go to the place from whence He came (John 8:14). He had an even stronger sense that His Father was with Him and in Him, and that He was never alone (John 8:16). He also declared that His indwelling Father was constantly bearing witness *within* Him to what He was saying and doing (John 8:18).

He had been sent *out* of the other realm into this one by His Father (John 8:26); and it was the Father who was in Him who was doing all the work (John 5:17).

Jesus Christ was with His Father while here on earth; He could see Him and hear Him. The only thing He spoke was what His Father first said to Him, and this pleased the Father (John 8:28, 38). He proceeded from (came out of) the Father (John 8:42; 7:28-29).

He stated that His followers would also be able to *hear* an indwelling God (John 8:47).

Jesus presently and experientially knew ("I *know*") the Father (John 8:55).

He could see Abraham seeing Him (John 8:56).

He could impart His life and the life of His Father to some of those who were of the fallen, third-place life form. He would give His life form in large quantity to those ones. Not a little of His life, but an abundance (John 10:10). His followers could then *hear* Him; even those not yet born would one day hear His voice. He knew which ones were those chosen people and which were not (John 10:11-18).

He could and would go back to the other realm. His enemies could not go there. He declared that He was *already* in the realm He was going to go to ("where I *am*"; John 7:34).

The Father has the highest form of life there is, and so does the Son; and some of the dead will hear His voice, rise, and *also receive this life* (John 5:26-29). He gives the highest life (John 10:28).

If you come to *Christ* (not Scripture, but Christ), *He* will give you *this* very life (John 5:39-40).

He said, "I did not originate in this realm. Everyone else did, but I did not. Refuse to believe me and you will never receive life, but will keep sin and death" (John 8:23-24).

"I am one with the Father. No one else is. But my followers will be one with Me" (John 10:30; John 17).

"I came out of the other realm as eatable bread. Eat *this bread* and have the highest life in you." Real bread is a *He,* not an *it,* and this bread is eternal (John 6:32-38).

He, and He alone, could see God; for He came from the Father to seek out the Father's own and give them life (John 6:46ff.).

And, of course, He stated that He lived by means of the life of His Father. Furthermore, the one who eats of Jesus Christ will have the same life in Him, and be able to live by that same life (John 6:57). He was speaking not of physical flesh, but of partaking of Christ's spirit, which spirit is eternal life (John 6:63).

Jesus knew from the outset who *would* and who *would not* believe (John 6:64-65).

When He spoke about "spirit," He spoke of his life. And when He spoke of his "life," He spoke of spirit. And the believer could have both in him. And the believer could live in that spirit and could live by means of that life (John 6:63).

Jesus Christ lived more by revelation, perception, and intuition—aspects of His divine life, rather than by intellect, willpower, and emotions. His disciples would also touch this way of living. It is possible to learn (to lay hold of) the way of "thinking" that belongs to the other realm (Matt. 16:17).

The other realm can be bound and made to obey a believer who stands here in this, our own realm (Matt. 16:19; 18:18).

There is another habitation where we will live (Luke 16:9).

It is what dwells deep inside a man that is all-important (Mark 7:15).

Perhaps the greatest fact we will lay hold of as Christians seeking to learn a deeper walk with the Lord is this: All spiritual experience of the Father radiates to the Son. Much of that spiritual experience that flows from the Father and is experienced by the Son *re-radiates* to the believer (John 10:15-16).

After the Lord resurrects the believer's spirit, that believer's spirit never tastes death again (John 11:25-26). The life in that spirit has already died and is risen again. So the believer's spirit and his new-found higher life will never taste death again! Jesus heard His Father from within, and His Father *also* heard Him from within. The Lord's vocal conversation with the Father was not necessary. Why? Theirs was a constant and ongoing fellowship that was *always* taking place, *inside* Jesus Christ (John 11:41-42).

By His death He would gather the elect and they would become children of God (John 11:52).

Jesus Christ, on occasion, related to His spirit by deep sighs, an experience that re-radiated to the believer (Mark 8:12; Rom. 8:26).

Jesus and His new creation are free of all obligation to the civilization of the fallen and third-highest life form; but they do conform on occasion, solely on the basis of not offending (Matt. 17:27; Rom. 15; Gal. 1–5).

These are only a few things that identify the uniqueness of the bio-*zoe*-ology of Jesus Christ. And remember, much of this uniqueness, by means of His redemptive work, re-radiates to you.

You presently, right now, have a right to the experience and reality of that realm (Eph. 1:2-3)!

A Look at Fallen Man's Soul

The fallen soul of Adam, fighting a valiant war but in the shadow of its pyre, would sometimes triumph over the encroachment of the flesh only to fall prey to its adversary at the very moment of victory.

Little by little, as the soul enlarged, the *mind* has sought to see, to understand, to duplicate—or failing that, to *counterfeit*—the ways of man's lifeless *spirit*.

And all the time the mind keeps up its taunting and jeering at the soul's emotions. The thinking apparatus is ever reminding the *emotions* that the mind is *superior* to *feelings*. And in believing its own false propaganda, the thinking mind finds itself living in a paradise reserved for fools.

The *will,* now set free from submission to the spiritual realm, seeks out its own niche—the triumph of human endeavors over all temptations and circumstances. And in so doing *will* gave birth, with *mind* as its accomplice, to the religion of success and accomplishment.

The *emotion,* ever the whipping boy of the *mind,* seeks thrills of ecstasy far beyond the capacity for which the soul was designed. Having pursued exotic thrills, *emotion* then falls back into despair, reaching depths of despondency far below any depths its Designer had created it to tolerate.

Seeking (but never reaching) those dimensions that are reserved for the spirit only, emotion joins will and mind to create a pale substitute for walking in the spirit's domain. These trilateral ingredients brewed together now bring forth just about the greatest curse man will ever know. This trinity that composes the damaged soul makes man *religious.* Then the soul informs man of one of the greatest of all deceptions. The soul tells man that his religious nature is actually his spiritual nature.

What has being religious done to man? Perhaps we can understand by recognizing fallen man's ability to produce religion.

Within the Christian faith, you will always find three "sub-religions." To recast that sentence: There are really only three denominations in Christendom. The *mind* denomination, the *emotion* denomination, and the *will* denomination. (Sometimes there is a combination of *two,* but *never* three!) Each of these three denominations sees itself as the *one* that is *spiritual.* And, of course, it *denominates* against the other two!

The fallen soul, it appears, is *very* sectarian.

Can you identify the three denominations within Christendom?

The mind denomination: Scholarly and theoretical, its ministers are expositors, well educated, strong on adherence to sound doctrine, strong on college and seminary education. Theology is everything. The ministers are cool, often to the point of being aloof, often so obsessed with the biblical that this one aspect becomes central to all else. Consequently, a living, intimate walk with Christ is often left outside, shivering in the cold.

Dare I give an example? Rather than naming them, most of these people fall into the lineage of either John Calvin, John Knox, or John Darby. (By the way, they are the folks who invented that world-famous, ever-challenged statement, "Don't trust your feelings.")

The emotional denomination: Boy, can these people sing! And worship! Unfortunately, they lack a bit in "pulpiteerism." The best way to go to church on Sunday morning is to come to one of these worship meetings at 11:00 A.M. and then, at 11:30, run like sixty to a "mindy" church. This way you will have the *best* of two *very* different, wholly incompatible worlds! Good singing and worship, and fantastic biblical exposition.

These emotion folks have fun! They shout; they praise; they press everything to the limit. Always there is the spectacular, but tragically, they are also ever in need of something more spectacular; therefore you will always find the latest fad in full swing here. And remember, if you ever start anything new that is exciting (and if it can possibly be labeled

Christian), *they* will steal it from you and make it *the* new work of God.

These folks enjoy being Christian, but they pay a terrible price: burnout! Burnout of the emotions, burnout on the spectacular, burnout on miracles, burnout on faith, and, as a result, an eventual distrust of anything, everything, and everybody attempting to take new territory for Christ.

Which are the emotions denominations? (Need I make a list?) The charismatic movement among evangelicals, the Catholic mystics among Roman Catholics, plus a lot of *non*denominational movements.

The will denomination: These fall into two categories. First there are the evangelists. "Evangelize the whole world, next weekend." Groups that are into *doing*—always soul winning. With a clear conscience I can call the name of one particular denomination because it is *my* denomination and therefore is *not* off limits to this author's pen: Southern Baptists. We have produced more evangelists than all other Protestant movements combined. We *will* evangelize the world.

The other category is the one that says, "You can *will* to live as a Christian." These are the legalists. They have a list of things you can and cannot do as a Christian. You will find them in *all* religious movements, for they are the carriers of the main element of all religion: "By my conduct and performance, I can win God's favor."

The combinations:

The thinker (mind) and the doer (will) combine to be very doctrinal and biblical *and* evangelistic. A formidable combination. These are almost always interdenominational groups.

The doer and the feeler (emotions): Much like the above, they are into evangelism, but they have more fun at it.

There is probably no thinker-feeler denomination. Those are natural enemies. That is, the mind denomination can't stand the emotion denomination.

The problem with all of the above? *All* are of the soul. The spirit operates on a level apart from think, feel, do. Mind, emotion, and will belong to the territory of the soul.

The Lord Jesus had all these aspects of the soul operating in Him, but in perfect balance. On the other hand, His primary life source was His spirit, *not* His soul. And in His spirit was the better way.

The Better Way

About one-third of us are predominantly thinkers, one-third of us are feelers, and one-third of us are doers. Must there be three denominations to accommodate us all? If sociologists are right, we are innately born with our dispositions. But the thinker wants the feeler to get logical; the doer wants both to straighten up and start evangelizing and/or to stop sinning; the feeler wants to be left to just love God and chase moonbeams, read poetry, perform miracles, see signs, get power, and watch sunsets.

Wisely, God had twelve different men to found the first ecclesia. All three dispositions were there, but all twelve men were drawing primarily from their spirits and not their dispositional souls. Would that the church could get a fresh, new start with twelve such men. (Your group—or church—probably reflects either the disposition of its founder or of your present leader.)

All three "denominations" put up a strong case for you not to have anything to do with the other two. ("God wants us to save souls, that's our only job." "What we have to do is get into the Book and memorize it." "Hey, there's a preacher down at the Garbonza Room of the Hillery Hotel who just had a vision that the world is going to turn into toothpaste next April 1.")

We look in hope to that day when the Lord's people lay down their dispositional differences we mistakenly view as doctrinal differences; return to being a community of believers; allow all dispositions to express themselves; learn tolerance of the others; and, most of all, operate as a corporate people from their *spirits,* thereby circumventing our irreconcilable soulical differences.

In the meantime . . .

A Kind Word to Those Who Trust Their Feelings

Theologians have had very little that was kind to say about the emoters.

Long before there were Protestants, the Catholic church tried to make room for all three of these denominational types under one umbrella. (They only partly succeeded.) There was philosophy and theology for the *mind* folks. There were missions and monkhood for the *doers* and the *legalists.* Then there were the Catholic mystics. Poor, unstable souls, they were forever being imprisoned, banished, or burned by the thinkers!

Luther came along (a doctorate in theology, a student of Augustine's philosophy, in fact an *Augustinian monk,* a . . . oh, never mind). Luther often declared that those Catholic mystics would *never* gain a toe in Lutheranism. Consequently, the Reformation was primarily an *intellectual* and theological reformation. It was an upheaval of theological and philosophical proportion. It was woefully lacking in revolution of spiritual depth and practical handles on the deeper walk with the Lord. And the Reformation desperately needed those elements but *never* got them. A deeper walk with Christ was never even birthed among the early Protestants. And if it had been, such a way of living surely would have been told to stand outside somewhere.

As luck would have it, about that time there came along something called the Muenster rebellion, which was a group of emoters gone completely off the deep end. And so it came about, the Protestant motto: "Don't trust your feelings. It is dangerous. You'll end up like the Muensters."

In all church history *that* was the only really big tragedy the emoters ever caused, and they have never been allowed to forget it. Christians by the millions have been conned by the *mindy* with the terrors of the Muenster story.

It is only fair to ask how dangerous it is to be a mindy, rational, intellectual, cool, controlled, logical Christian. There have been several hundred wars in Europe fought over doctrinal disputes. Millions have been killed in those wars. Do you really believe the emoters did *that?* It was biblical doctrine, pamphlets, speeches, books, and debates wrung from the greatest minds of Christendom who were the seedlings and promoters of those wars. Millions of believers have been injured, enslaved, tortured, and murdered by other Christians. It was all over the intellectual, rational, logical doctrinal differences of the mindy.

You might find it interesting to read the accounts of . . . oh, take the Huguenots. Read about them in dungeons, tied on racks, being roasted over fires, scalding lead poured in their mouths, eyes gouged out, women in birth pangs with their legs tied together while mother and child died in unbelievable agony. In each case a theologian, with Bible in hand, then stood beside the tortured soul seeking rationally to convince him or her that the intelligent thing to do was recant.

Those are real stories. And the deeds were not done at the hand of feelers, but verse-quoting thinkers who rationalized with mind and Scripture that what they were doing (torturing and killing) was *Christian.*

But that was a darker age. What of ours? Today, see hot-hearted young men burning for Christ enter post-graduate study in a seminary, there to be filled with the academics of two thousand years, and come out three years later so soaked in "mindiness" that they are almost unfit to serve Christ in the real world.

Walk the aisles of your bookstore; see the daggers and spears within the pages of those books aimed at other children of God who differ with them. The feelers and doers didn't write those books, found those institutions, nor throw those spears. The thinkers did that.

The point is simple. The whole soul fell. Your spirit is not located in your emotions. Your emotions are fallen. But not one bit more fallen and not a bit less trustable than your thinking mind. The logic, reasoning, rationale, dialectics, and cognition of your mind (even in its grave ponderings of the Bible) are not one whit more trustworthy than someone else's emotions. *Both intellect and emotions are fallen!* Seriously fallen.

But what of that verse, 2 Timothy 1:7, about having a sound mind?

God has given you
the *spirit* of a sound mind.

There is only *one* sound mind. It is your Lord's! His mind is *in* your spirit, *not* in your mind and/or your emotions. Reread the verse. God gave you a spirit. *His* spirit. In His spirit is a sound mind. *His* mind.

Finally, be encouraged, dear emoter. The Lord had twelve disciples. The ranks of the twelve contained both the mindy, the willful, the emotional, and all the usual combinations thereof. When someone tells you not to trust your emotions, remind him which of those twelve men the Lord chose as their leader. Peter may have been a doer. He may have been a feeler, but no one will ever say that spontaneous, miracle-working, illiterate fisherman was a mindy thinker. God chose a trigger-happy ignorare to be the leader of the primitive ecclesia!

Think about that, dear thinker!

What about Paul? Which was he?

Maybe a doer. He certainly was a legalist by

nature, a world traveler, evangelist, and church planter. A feeler? He cried his way across the empire. A thinker? He wrote some of the best Christian literature ever penned. Which was he? Just possibly a man who lived on the other side of his natural human disposition. Perhaps a man who lived by means of his spirit.

Pagan Philosophy and Its View of Man's Soul

Take Your Choice

Nonbiblical Writers

"Man is body and soul; the soul of man is that part of him that is spiritual."—Plato

"Man is body and soul."—Aristotle

"Man is body and soul."—Augustine

"Man is body and soul; the soul of man is that part of him that is spiritual."—Pseudo-Dionysius

"Man is body and soul; the soul of man is that part of him that is spiritual."—Thomas Aquinas

"Man is body and soul."—Martin Luther

"Man is body and soul."—Huldrych Zwingli

"Man is body and soul."—John Calvin

"Man is body and soul."—*The Baptist Commentary*

Now, I realize that I may be wrong, but it seems to me there is an outside possibility that somewhere around here we may have overlooked something that just might be very important.—Gene Edwards

Biblical Sources

"The spirit of man is the lamp of God."—David

"The Lord forms the spirit of man within him."—Zechariah

"My spirit has rejoiced in God."—Mary

"He that is born of the Spirit is spirit."—Jesus Christ

"The words I speak to you are spirit and life."—Jesus Christ

"The life I live, I live by means of my Father. My Father is Spirit."—Jesus Christ

"Serve your employer with all your soul."—Paul

"May your spirit and soul and body be sanctified."—Paul

Why have we heard so little on this central issue of man's being *spirit,* as well as soul and body? Why is man seen almost universally as body and soul? Why an almost total void of any reference to man as partly spirit? Why so little known about the human spirit? Why, for most of the last 1,700 years, have scholarly Christians been teaching that we are body and soul, when we are actually spirit, soul, and body?

Well, the problem all started in *places* you probably never thought of, among men you probably never heard of. Parmenides? Zeno? Pythagoras, Anaxagoras, Heraclitus? (You *have* heard of Pythagorus. In the ninth grade. It had something to do with a right triangle, a sum of two sides, and a theorem.)

All those men listed above were of Greek origin, and they were all heathen. They are the grandfathers of a (pagan) school of Western thought called the *Pythagorean school of philosophy.* One of these fellows, in his interminable speculations, began to conjecture on the subject *What is man?* He concluded that man was body and soul. And so it stuck. And *every* philosopher since has accepted that view and speculated on what "soul" meant.

The person who cemented this idea into the thought of Western man was a short, fat, dumpy, lazy, bald-headed little man who couldn't support his wife and children, and who was fond of driving people crazy with his questions. He probably had one of the highest IQs ever known to mankind. Given the fact he was driving the city fathers to distraction and the rumor he was leading the young men who were his disciples into homosexuality, he was sentenced to die by having to drink some foul-tasting poison. This little man, Socrates by name, and two of his followers became the most influential people in the history of Western thinking.*

In one of those quirks of history, all three of the above-mentioned philosophers weighed in with some of the highest IQs of all time. (The youngest of the three men may very well have had *the* highest IQ in human history.) All three men taught, "Man is body and soul." Their writings, to this very day, are held as

---

* Some might say the Lord Jesus and the apostle Paul had a greater influence on Western man, but perhaps the *greatest* single influence of these three Greek philosophers is in their corruption of the Christian faith!

almost sacred throughout the earth. Their influence on all our lives is nothing less than staggering.*

Their teaching should have simply been passed around in the circles of high-IQ heathen philosophers. No such luck. Their profound ideas certainly should never have come over into the Christian faith! But they did! And there is an excellent chance the Christian faith at large will never recover from this sad event.

Long before, the Hebrew prophets had seen man as a whole. But they also knew that, within that wholeness of man, he was a spirit, a soul, and a body.

Jesus Christ had no teaching on this matter at all. He *is* Truth. He had reality as His experience, not teachings. He was whole—with a spirit, soul, and body there within His wholeness. His experience was also the experience of His followers. Man has a body, and it interfaces with man's soul; man is a soul, but the soul interfaces with man's spirit. Soul and spirit so interlock that *only* an indwelling Lord can distinguish soul from spirit.

Man's humanity rests in his soul. The Lord Jesus' main place of residence in the believer is in his spirit.

Heathen philosophers had absolutely no idea of such a view. They could not have comprehended such a thing had they heard it. The Christians had cared less what those heathen believed. But the heathen philosophers of the second and third centuries who became believers perpetrated this view on fellow Christians. One of these diametrically opposed views had to go. Unfortunately the idea of man as "body

---

* It has been said, "A person born in the West cannot think unless he thinks Aristotle." That proposition has never been seriously challenged.

and soul" won out over "spirit, soul, and body." Probably forever.

It happened on this wise: Around the middle of the second century (c. A.D. 150), a few philosophers, all of them "sons" of Plato and Aristotle, began to convert to Christianity. They came into the Christian faith bringing their philosophical and pagan mindset with them. Unfortunately, a few of them picked up the powerful pen. Other Christians living during that time appear to have been too busy being Christians to write anything. The fact that the writings of these pagan philosophers-turned-Christian are about all that survived as "Christian" literature during this era gives a terribly distorted view of what second-century Christianity was like.

Having not paid a lot of attention to the deep (spiritual) things of our faith, and having paid a great deal of attention to the *profound* things of Greco-heathon philosophy, these philosophers-turned-Christian began applying the dialectics and logic of Aristotle to the analysis of the Christian faith. In so doing, they offhandedly declared man to be soul and body. This was, after all, the only view concerning man that they had ever heard of. The Christian faith might have been untouched by this corruption except for two men. Make that *three* men. These men were all steeped in Greco-heathen philosophy *and* at the same time they claimed to be Christian (and probably were).

I may lose you in the next few paragraphs, but these facts *really* need to be in print.

We will begin with a brilliant young teenager named Origen. As a youth, he loved to learn. And while still very young, he also learned that he loved to teach. What were the influences that had flowed into his head? First, there was the Socratic line of philosophy (Socrates—Plato—Aristotle—Philo).

The second major philosophical line that molded Origen's life was Stoicism and a touch of Neo-Pythagoreanism (Antisthenes—Zeno of Citium—Panaetius—Sation—Seneca—Epicletus).

But the most important influence of all pouring into his high IQ was a philosophy called Neoplatonism. And like it or not, this philosophy *still* dominates a large part of Christian theology and is a major factor in the mind-set of all modern-day Christians.

The *first* ingredient in Neoplatonism is a blend of (1) Neo-Pythagoreanism, (2) the Socratic school, and (3) Stoicism. Put all these together, shake them up, and out comes something referred to as the philosophy of *self-realization*. For Origen, there was yet one more influence that shaped him. He sat under a teacher named Plotinus. Shake all these concoctions and out comes Neoplatonism.

Now, take a little of the influence of a fellow named Tertullian, add the writings of Paul and other early Christian writings (all filtered through the analysis of Aristotelian dialectics), and you have coming out of Origen something called *religious* Neoplatonism.

The Christian faith was about to get into *big* trouble. After Origen died, his teachings became very popular among pagan philosophers-turned-Christian. And remember, all of them offhandedly referred to man as body and soul. No one noticed that the Christian faith was losing spiritual depth and that this loss was being replaced with the profundity of philosophy.

During this era the leaders of the Christian faith were wild-eyed *church planters* similar to the first century *ecclesia planters*. But gradually the direction of our faith moved into the hands of intellectual speculators. (We would do our faith the greatest of all boosts if we would return to being led by wild-eyed church planters.) That is, the leaders of the faith gradually became men who spoke, theorized, and conjectured somewhere out in the upper stratosphere of the outer cerebral hemisphere.

It has been suggested that it takes an IQ of at least 130 to clearly follow the abstract reasoning of Greek philosophers. It requires an IQ of 140 to knowledgeably converse in its finer details and defend or attack them. An IQ of 150 or over is needed in order to add anything new to the philosophical legacy.

That leaves over 95 percent of the human race *out*. The Christian faith has been led primarily by speculative men of extremely high IQ for over a millennium. Those are not the kind of men our Lord intended to be the pacesetters and leaders of our faith. Where are those wild-eyed *church planters,* anyway?

Unfortunately, it is also from men with IQs of 130 and above that we usually recruit our seminary and Bible school professors. They in turn mold the preachers of tomorrow. Generally speaking, such men love to ascend into the upper atmosphere of dialectic conjurings. They call it "theological discussions." Because such men have traditionally trained both our Protestant and Catholic ministers, we have suffered incalculable *spiritual* loss.

Among other things, the concept of man as *body and soul* reigns unquestioned in theological circles to this very day.

Furthermore, plunging a hot-hearted young man, called of God, into the rarefied atmosphere of the dialectics of philosophy gives him an intellectual "high" that is *often* mistaken for spiritual depth, spiritual insight, and spiritual experience. (It ain't!) The influence of all these things on our faith and our ministries has been incredibly disproportionate, unnecessary, and *very* destructive.

Our story continues.

One of the men influenced by the writings of Origen was a gentleman named Augustine (c. A.D. 400). But other teachings also influenced Augustine: Manichaeism and Asceticism, plus Origen's Neoplatonism, plus Philo. (Philo was a *Hebrew* teacher, so add Hebrew thought strained through Aristotle's philosophy to Augustine's mind-set.)

Augustine had one other influence in his life. A mother, named Monica, who gave him a somewhat Judeo-Christian heritage.

Augustine taught a strong Platonic philosophy, sprinkled with some Aristotle. Of course, he presented man as *body and soul*. This is crucial: It became church dogma that Augustinian intellectualism was the best way to know spiritual things. To know Christ deeply, master Augustine. Intellectualism and spirituality are one and the same! It was that simple, that intellectual, and that nonspiritual. That dogma has stuck for 1,600 years. This is true of both Catholics and Protestants, though Protestants are generally not as aware of these theological roots as educated Catholics are.

The writings of Augustine were elevated almost to the point of being as inspired as Scriptures—at least by Catholics. His influence on Christianity is titanic. Without a blink, he taught what Aristotle and Plato taught, that man was body and soul. For him, that settled the issue.

The roots of Augustinianism (sometimes called Platonic dualism) look something like this: Pythagoras Socrates Plato Stoicism Philo Plotinus Clement Numenius Origen.

The next ingredients of Augustinianism follow thusly: Platonism Speusippus Arcesilaus Carneades The Academies (Skepticism).

The last influence on Augustine's thinking looked like this: Plato Saccas Plotinus (Neoplatonism).

Shake all that up and you get *religious Neoplatonic Dualism.* (Clear as mud, eh?)

Somewhere in there we lost the deeper Christian life to the abstractions of high IQs: "Intellectualism *is* spirituality."

Impressed?

Perhaps we could have survived even all of this had it not been for the next man. His influence on the Christian faith will curse us until the crack of doom. Enter a nameless fraud who called himself Dionysius the Areopagite.

Now, there had been a *real* Dionysius who had lived during the first century, in Greece. Paul of Tarsus led him to Christ. But this fellow who later claimed to be Dionysius was a *fifth-century* monk living in Syria. He was cranking out literature that he was claiming was *first*-century writing. In other words, he was a *lying* fraud.

This rascal was enamored with the Neoplatonic philosophy, which was in vogue at the time. He wrote as though he had lived during the first century. Furthermore, he stated that Timothy sat at his feet! (Timothy had been dead over four hundred years when Dionysius made this claim.)

When people read his writings, they really thought they were looking at a profound Christian who was a personal friend and student of Paul. They thought Paul was, therefore, a Neoplatonic Christian philosopher-theologian. It was nearly a thousand years before this hoax was finally rejected. By then the damage was done, and it was irreversible. This man's ideas are warp and woof of the Christian faith. You don't believe?

Here is but one example of his influence.

Every time you see a steeple, or stained-glass window, or high-vaulted ceiling in a church, you are seeing the philosophy of this man in physical expression.

Plato had taught that color, light, space, and beauty could aid in bringing a person into oneness with the "other than"; that man could employ such things to help him come "into touch with the sublime."

Men who wanted to build grand church buildings quoted Dionysius—the supposed friend of Paul—thinking they had a first-century "proof text" to justify steeples, high-vaulted ceilings, and stained-glass windows as scriptural. They were, of course, actually quoting a quacky, fifth-century Plato revisionist! Remember that the next time you pass a church building! Pseudo-Dionysius (the name by which he is called today), this obscure desert monk (c. A.D. 500), enamored with the fad philosophy of his day, turned that fad into one of the main pillars of Christian theology. It is a philosophy-theology that is *still* a major influence on Christian thought.

His work is riddled with heathen philosophy that is just barely couched in Christian vocabulary. A modification of Plato's thought ruled his writings. For a thousand years, learned theologians quoted this man, thinking they were quoting a *major first-century Christian* figure.

But herein lies the greatest tragedy of Dionysius.

Enter a man named Tom!

The world's other great IQ, a fellow named Thomas Aquinas (d. 1274), immortalized a synthesis of Augustine and Dionysius. It is said, "Thomas Aquinas baptized Aristotle and made him a good Catholic." He also baptized Plato while he was at it. How? Well, Aquinas quoted Dionysius—as a first-century Christian source—*over* one hundred times in his massive work of biblical theology!

That theological work, its foundations resting on the writings of Dionysius, has been summed up this way:

> Thomas Aquinas took Augustine, the early Christian writings, adapted the Neoplatonic theme, and turned it all into a Christian philosophical-theological *worldview.* He harmonized the *major insights* and doctrines of the Platonic, Aristotelian and

Neoplatonic lines of thought, and then made them Christian.

What has that to do with you? And me?

Aquinas's teachings were made the *official* doctrines of the Catholic church. If Aquinas said it, then it was reality and truth. Ah, but *you* are not a Catholic. Well, I vividly recall one of my seminary professors saying, "Thomas Aquinas is *the* most influential theologian in church history, among both Catholics and Protestants. The books we teach from and the books we write in the area of systematic theology still follow his format."

Read it and weep, dear Christian.

Finally, to drive the last nail in the coffin of a spiritual walk with Christ first-century style, we come to a young Augustinian monk (a true son of the teachings of Augustine). He took the Augustinian teachings, peppered with the synthesism of Thomastic theology, and created *Protestant theology.*

The monk's name was Martin Luther.

So Aquinas's theology reigns today as the theological root of all Catholic and Protestant theology. Please hear Aquinas's view on the subject of body and soul.

> The human soul is created in direct relation to the prime matter it individualizes. The soul is the unity of the composite human substance. It is the principle of all man's operations.
>
> The highest faculty of the soul is the *intellectual. The intellectual aspect of the soul is the soul's spiritual* faculty. It is the

intellectual aspect of the soul that is capable of transcendental realities.

Now you know where the idea that man is only a body and soul came from.

Just how bad off are we?

Virtually every Christian commentary ever written takes up the theme that man is body and soul, and is flavored with the view of the soul as seen by Thomas Aquinas. This leaves us all in an ambiguous place; we see the soul as "human," yet with something spiritual about it. We end up seeing phraseology like, "man's indomitable spirit of courage," and "the soul of man returning to its spiritual essence."

But the saddest part is not only the loss of the spirit, but the fact that the intellect of man is that which is seen as his most spiritual part. No wonder we have no idea of what "the spirituals" means. An indwelling Lord simply has no place anywhere in all these writings. The subject virtually never comes up. An understanding of the human spirit's being one with God's Spirit exists almost wholly in 1 Corinthians and never in theology. In a world where man is but body and soul, to attempt to understand and experience the Christian's spiritual side is to end up bumping into the mind-set of Western man.

Furthermore, this dichotomous concept of man appears to be forever entwined in the mind of Western man.

Moreover, when psychiatry and psychology entered into Christian theology (by way of something dubiously called "Christian counseling"), it also carried with it the pagan/heathen humanistic concept of man as body and soul. At that point, the battle, it seems, was forever lost.

Christian counseling, self-centric by its very nature, has left us trying to solve soul problems with the soul! That may sound reasonable, but most of our problems of the soul will be solved only within our spiritual faculties. Christian terms such as "the centrality of Christ" and "the cross" are used in Christian counseling, but the use of these words reflects little or nothing of the original spiritual meaning.

The *proper abode* for the believer is a difficult matter for man to lay hold of. "To walk in your spirit" and to "live in your spirit" began way back two thousand years ago as terms that came out of experience—experience that was real. Communicating that reality across twenty centuries and several thousand dead philosophers is not easy.

Using a seemingly spiritual vocabulary does not give us access to the spiritual realm. We may hear the words, but our mind-set is still thinking in terms of man's soul being his spiritual seat. We may speak of the spirituals forever, but to no avail if we do not know how to touch that realm.

Should this planet last another three thousand years, men will still be teaching Christians that they are body and soul. Aristotle is that *deeply* entrenched in Christian theology.

It was not until the twentieth century that a lady named Mary McDonough and a man named T. Austin Sparks pointed out that we are spirit, soul, and body. Until then, almost no one had noticed the cavernous disparity. Even then men looked, thought, and soberly declared, "Perhaps there is a difference in soul and spirit, but whatever the difference, it is of no great significance."

Not significant? Only the difference between Jesus' life and our life. The difference between this realm and the realm of the spiritual. Only the difference in our Adamic inheritance and our divine inheritance.

Unless there is a radical change from the last 1,700 years of church history, an indwelling Lord and the highest life will probably remain a territory populated by desperate and thirsty believers. That is, by believers who have dropped *everything* in quest of knowing Him. A tiny group indeed.

But that is probably as it should be.

The Habitat after Constantine

After the third century a very corrupt version of the *community* of the believers was carried on by *monks* out in deserts and on isolated mountains. There they pursued God and called the corporate, isolated, celibate life the best way to pursue God. When *that* mind-set prevailed, the true nature of the ecclesia seemed to have disappeared from recorded history.

It is a titanic undertaking to try to explain that this original corporateness is an *indispensable* ingredient to "living the Christian life." How titanic? My guess is that it will take another two hundred years before a really workable, practical, corporate experience of the ecclesia finds its way into the life of the majority of evangelicals. Or perhaps three or four hundred years. And I am an optimist! And if you *think* that is a pessimistic view, then consider just how little the *practice* of our faith has changed since the Reformation. Very little, and the Reformation happened over four hundred years ago.

Where is the evangelical mind today as concerns the link between a deeper walk with Christ and the need of the ecclesia? We have all read or heard the story of John Bunyan's immortal classic, *The Pilgrim's Progress.* But Bunyan did not serve the kingdom of God well when he forever gave us the stereotype of the Christian seeker. Here is Pilgrim, the consummate evangelical believer, dauntless and *alone,* setting out to discover the riches of Christ *all by himself.* He has been "dauntless" and "alone" ever since.

Getting to know Christ in the depths is virtually always presented to us as an individual pursuit. It is a noncorporate, almost hermitlike picture of the seeker. No wonder all our formulas do not work. As the great evangelical individualistic believer living outside a corporate expression of the ecclesia, the seeker will remain a seeker until doomsday. Unless, while out there in a trackless wilderness, he happens to accidentally stumble upon his natural habitat.

Please understand me. A steepled building that opens its doors sharply at 11:00 on Sunday morning (an absolutely dreadful hour to pick for a religious gathering) and closes those doors sharply at 12:05 just isn't the first century believers' concept of our species' habitat.

What is more, listen carefully to what is being said in that building and you will notice that even though the message is being delivered to an audience, it is being addressed to the *individual.* Listen!

The message is not delivered to a corporate community. How often have you heard a message on a *corporate* quest to know and experience Jesus Christ in the depths? The message you hear may be given in a room containing many people, but the content is aimed totally at you, the *isolated* soul. No such thing ever happened in the first century. "Individual" is our mind-set today. "Corporate" was their mind-set then.

My own observation, dear reader, is that we have a long way to go before *ecclesia* means to us evangelicals, *experientially,* what it meant to the founders of our faith.

And expect the emphasis on individualism to grow, as more and more psychology is introduced into the Sunday morning sermon.

Yes, from where we are now it may be two hundred years before evangelicals lay hold of the corporate nature of our faith. And if pop psychology continues its inroads at its present pace, our *individual* needs may become the only message we ever hear. If that happens, forget two hundred years and make it seven hundred years!

One of the most incredible things we can observe in our lifetime is to see just how far afield the body of Christ can move from its foundation; from being a habitat, a city, a house, a nation, where believers are constantly in contact with one another, day in and day out. So far afield are we from that, yet how many of us are filled with a longing for so much more than we have—every cell in our bodies crying out for spiritual reality, for a home, for the habitat of our species.

But it takes a hardy believer to set out on such an uncharted course. Who among us has not quailed as we have heard solemnly intoned to us, *"Do not forsake* the assembling of yourselves together." (Why is it that every time we hear the statement, 11:00 on Sunday morning flashes into our minds?) One thing is sure, when the seeking Christian begins to entertain the idea that traditional Sunday rituals just may not be enough to satisfy the believer, he will be warned to "not forsake the assembling together." With that verse we get scared, and stay where we are.

It is up to you, dear reader, to decide for yourself whether or not sitting on a pew in a big auditorium at 11:00 on Sunday morning is the *natural* habitat of your species.

The Fundamental Error of Legalism

Good is not the issue you have to struggle with. "Being good" is certainly not God's measurement. Morals are not the issue. Run after decency, rules, rights, morality, modesty, honesty, and right living . . . until you are half mad with despair, yet you will never satisfy the drive in you "to be good " Never! And despite your greatest efforts, you will never see others, whom you demand "be good," do anything but *fail*. They, living under your rules, will never live up to your demands of them. Beating your head on a stone holds more hope of accomplishing something positive than does your demand for right conduct. No matter how moral you are, you will never quiet that voice within you that cries out, "Do better! You haven't quite gone far enough!" Or, "Do better! This is not high enough!"

I recommend that you do what the greatest legalist of all time did. Do like St. Simon did. Climb up a fifty-foot stone pillar, perch yourself up there on a space three feet square, eat a daily ration consisting solely of three figs per day. Do this for your entire adult life. And *still* something inside you will cry out, "Make your living space two feet square. Eat two figs per day! And shame on you for what you dreamed last night. And just think how terrible was the thought you had this morning. Obviously you are utterly unworthy. Try harder!"

Do all St. Simon did, and you are living still in the biosphere of the tree (and its knowledgeable fruit) that is evil *and* good. The drive to be *good* comes from the tree of tyranny, rules, legalism, performance, evil, *and* good. The Tree of Death!

Life and freedom come from a wholly different tree. Victory is in life, not good. Triumph is in freedom, not in standards.

The tree from which Adam did *not* eat was not called the Tree of *Good*. It was called Life.

Gene Edwards can be reached at:
Message Ministry
P.O. Box 18203
Atlanta, Georgia 30316

The second volume of this Introduction to the Deeper Christian Life is entitled *The Secret to the Christian Life* and is published by Tyndale House Publishers.